Africans in America

THE SPREAD OF PEOPLE AND CULTURE

CATHERINE REEF

☑ Facts On File, Inc.

Africans in America: The Spread of People and Culture

Copyright © 1999 by Catherine Reef

All rights reserved. No part of this book may be reproduced or utilized in any form or by any means, electronic or mechanical, including photocopying, recording, or by any information storage or retrieval systems, without permission in writing from the publisher. For information contact:

Facts On File, Inc.
11 Penn Plaza
New York NY 10001

Library of Congress Cataloging-in-Publication Data

Reef, Catherine.
    Africans in America : the spread of people and culture / Catherine Reef.
        p.   cm.—(Library of African-American history)
    Includes bibliographical references (p.   ) and index.
    Summary: Describes the spread of Africans to the western hemisphere and the influences and development of their culture.
    ISBN 0-8160-3772-8 (acid-free paper)
    1. Africans—America—History—Juvenile literature. 2. America—Civilization—African influences—Juvenile literature. 3. African diaspora—juvenile literature. [1. Africans—America—History. 2. America—Civilization—African influences. 3. Africa—Emigration and immigration.] I. Title. II. Series.
E29.N3R42 1999
970'.00496—dc21   98-11793

Facts On File books are available at special discounts when purchased in bulk quantities for businesses, associations, institutions or sales promotions. Please call our Special Sales Department in New York at (212) 967-8800 or (800) 322-8755.

You can find Facts On File on the World Wide Web at http://www.factsonfile.com

Text design by Cathy Rincon
Cover design by Nora Wertz
Layout by Robert Yaffe
Map on page 8 by Dale Williams

Printed in the United States of America

MP FOF 10 9 8 7 6 5 4 3 2

This book is printed on acid-free paper.

Contents

Introduction

African people jour-
neyed to foreign continents long before the 16th century and
the start of New World slavery. African merchants and sailors
visited the shores of Europe and the Middle East beginning
in the 10th century. Africans accompanied European crusad-
ers in the 11th, 12th, and 13th centuries to fight for control
of Jerusalem and other holy places.

As early as the eighth century, North Africans and Arabs
traded in slaves from lands south of the Sahara Desert. This
commerce would continue for 1,500 years, and it would
carry Africans to lands as far away as India, China, and
Japan. The slaves mined salt in the Persian Gulf region and
dove for pearls off the coast of Bahrain. Today, there are
communities in Pakistan, India, Iraq, and Iran that trace their
ancestry to enslaved Africans.

The largest migration from Africa, however, and the one with the greatest impact on world history and culture, began soon after Christopher Columbus reached the New World, in the late 15th century. From that time until well into the 1800s, about 12 million* Africans were brought to the Americas on slave ships. Europeans arrived in large numbers as well. Colonization of the New World caused the largest relocation of people—both black and white, African and European—that the world had ever seen. Never before had so many people from different cultural backgrounds interacted so closely.

The term *African diaspora* refers to this spread of African people and culture that resulted from the European slave trade. An understanding of the diaspora—where Africans went in the New World and how they influenced cultures there—forms a basis for the study of African-American history.

For many years, historians maintained that slavery robbed the Africans of their heritage: African-American culture, if such a thing existed, came about through borrowing from, and mimicking, whites. "The Negro, when he landed in the United States, left behind him almost everything but his dark complexion and his tropical temperament," one scholar wrote in 1919. Alain Locke, a distinguished black professor, asserted 17 years later that "slavery not only physically transplanted the Negro; it cut him off sharply from his cultural roots . . . and reduced him, so to speak, to a cultural zero."

Such statements clearly belong to the past. As interest in African-American history grew in the second half of the 20th century, so did our understanding of the African contribution to American civilization.

---

* Experts disagree on the exact number, but the most accurate current estimate is 11,863,000, cited in Ronald Segal's *The Black Diaspora* (1995) and John Iliffe's *Africans: The History of a Continent* (1995).

In recent decades, social scientists have compared the lives of West Africans with those of their descendants across the Atlantic Ocean. They have found many *Africanisms,* or African influences, in American life. An Africanism can be something obvious, such as a folk tale transported largely intact. More likely, though, an Africanism is subtle: an approach to prayer, perhaps, or a way of phrasing a song.

Another term, *Africanization,* refers to Africans leaving their mark on the larger society. Africanization is most apparent in coastal Brazil and in the Caribbean, the two regions to which most of the enslaved Africans were transported, although it occurred throughout the New World.

Earlier scholars may have missed the African influences on American culture because of their focus: They were looking for exact duplication of life in Africa. Today, we know that no people can transport their customs, values, and beliefs from one place to another without having them change. A new climate, strange animals and plants, encounters with different populations—any number of factors force people to adapt their way of life to a new setting.

Because enslaved Africans lived under white domination, they had less power to carry on their traditions than other immigrant groups did. Yet they managed to give their lives meaning. They kept some control over their beliefs, their rituals, and their means of self-expression. Wherever they were taken—to South or Central America, to the West Indies, or to the United States—they forged unique cultures that drew on both the past and the present. Their labor made it possible to settle and develop the Western Hemisphere. Their contributions to spoken language and literature, to music and dance, to art and religion, have enriched life for the entire population.

People of African descent continued to move and to influence culture after slavery was abolished. In the United States, the flow of people known as the Great Migration brought thousands of southern blacks to the North between

1910 and 1940. Following World War II, many descendants of slaves moved from the West Indies to Great Britain or the United States. In recent years, practitioners of the African-influenced religion Santería have fled Cuba for New York City and Miami, Florida.

African Americans have also reached back to Africa to renew ties with their ancestral homeland. Some have tried to establish settlements on the African continent, where descendants of slaves might escape American racism. Marcus Garvey's founding of the Black Star Steamship Line in 1919 was such an effort. Historically black colleges and universities in the United States have trained Africans in disciplines important to their developing nations. Cooperative ventures are now under way between American and African colleges. Finally, at sites in Tennessee, New York City, and elsewhere, archaeologists are learning more about the first Africans in the New World.

And so the African diaspora thrives. According to a proverb that has come to us from the Ashanti people of West Africa, "Ancient things remain in the ears." Long-held beliefs and time-honored practices—the distant memories that buzzed in the ears of enslaved people—remain strong themes in the music of American life.

NOTES

p. viii "The Negro, when he landed . . ." Robert Park, "The Conflict and Fusion of Cultures with Special Reference to the Negro," *Journal of Negro History*" (April 1919), p. 116.

p. viii "slavery not only . . ." Alain Locke, *Negro Art: Past and Present* (1936; New York: Arno Press and the *New York Times*, 1969), p. 2.

p. x "Ancient things remain . . ." Quoted in Mary Frances Berry and John W. Blassingame, *Long Memory: The Black Experience in America* (New York: Oxford University Press, 1982), p. 32.

1

The Treasure House

The West African Heritage

On the eve of the 16th century, the kings and queens of Europe sent fleets of sailing ships across the Atlantic with an eye to discovery and to gain. The lush vegetation of the Caribbean islands bespoke fertile land and a warm, moist climate for farming. The native people of the Americas wore ornaments of precious metal that hinted of greater riches to be mined from the earth. In 1500, following his third voyage of exploration, Christopher Columbus declared that he had found "the spot of earthly paradise." Nowhere had he come upon such abundant fresh water or constant mild temperatures as on the islands of Cuba and Hispaniola, which he had claimed for Spain.

Europe Colonizes the New World

Columbus opened a new world to European colonization and trade. Spanish forces conquered Mexico in 1519 and Peru in 1526. The Portuguese reached Brazil in 1500 and established a colony there. In the 17th century, France seized Guadeloupe, Martinique, and the western third of Hispaniola. The English and Dutch founded colonies on some of the smaller Caribbean islands and on the North American mainland.

The Europeans exploited the region's most valuable resource, its people. They enslaved the Indians and forced them to clear land for farming and to mine silver, gold, and emeralds.

The native population adapted poorly to slavery. Harsh treatment and European diseases wiped out the Borinqueño Indians of Puerto Rico, the Ciboney people of Cuba, and other ethnic groups. Scholars have estimated that 3 million Caribs lived on Hispaniola when Columbus reached the island in the 1490s. By 1549, Hispaniola's native population numbered only 28,000. In addition, those Indians who fought against European control, including some nomadic people of Brazil, suffered heavy losses in battle.

Faced with a waning native population and a constant need for laborers, the Europeans brought in captives from another region they had been exploring: the west coast of Africa.

Portugal had established a chain of settlements along the African coast in the 15th century for the purpose of trading. "These pioneers found Africa to be a treasure house," writes historian Benjamin Quarles. Africa yielded wealth in the form of gold, ivory, and slaves. In the 1460s, Portugal was transporting more than 700 slaves to Europe every year. Some of those Africans crossed the Atlantic as crew members with Columbus, Vasco Núñez de Balboa, and other explorers. In 1511, the Spanish crown dispatched the first major contingent of enslaved Africans, 50 in number, to the Caribbean colonies.

Africans Labor in the Americas

From 1511 onward, over the course of more than three centuries, the number of slaves in the New World steadily multiplied. The first to come were *ladinos,* or Africans who had been living in Portugal or Spain. To keep up with the demand for labor, empire-building nations soon were transporting slaves directly from Africa. The enslaved people raised sugar and other crops in the Caribbean and in Brazil, and they mined gold on Puerto Rico. Mining was the principal work for slaves in Mexico, or New Spain. Two important factors contributed to the steady rise in the enslaved African population. First, the Africans showed more resistance to European diseases than the Indians did. Second, the Africans were less likely to run away or secure weapons than the Indians were, because they were working in a strange land.

In all, as many as 12 million Africans journeyed to the Americas between the 16th and 19th centuries. Nearly two-thirds were men. Few children were captured in the first centuries of the slave trade, but by 1800, boys as young as 10 made up a large part of the ships' cargoes. Most enslaved workers went to the Caribbean and Central and South America, and especially to Brazil, the destination of about 5 million. Only 45 of every 1,000 African-born slaves came ashore on the Atlantic coast of North America.

In some colonies, enslaved Africans outnumbered Europeans. The island of Barbados, which was colonized by the English, was a notable example. In 1645, a visitor named George Downing noted that the Barbadian sugar planters

A crew member sailing with Sir Francis Drake made this drawing of enslaved Africans mining gold in 16th-century Central America. The Africans wash the gold, dry it over a fire, and present it to a Spanish overseer. (The Pierpont Morgan Library, New York. MA 3900, f.100)

"have bought this year no lesse than a thousand Negroes; and the more they buie, the better able they are to buye. For in a yeare and a halfe they will earne (with gods blessing) as much as they cost." Slave labor was cheap and profitable. By 1712, there were 41,970 enslaved Africans on Barbados and only 12,528 free citizens.

Portugal dominated the slave trade at first, docking its ships at Luanda in West-central Africa. As Christians, the Portuguese faced a moral dilemma because their faith taught them that slavery was wrong. They soon found that they could ease their consciences, though, by baptizing their captives. The Portuguese told themselves that the Africans benefited from enslavement. "For though their bodies were now brought into some subjection, that was a small matter in comparison of their souls, which would now possess true freedom for ever more," noted a Portuguese scribe.

England started supplying the New World with slaves in the 1550s. By the middle of the 18th century, England had surpassed Portugal to become the world's major slave-trading nation. Holland was drawn into the slave trade as well, using the port city of Loango, north of the Congo River, as the hub of its trading activity. France, Denmark, Sweden, the German state of Brandenburg, and England's North American colonies also trafficked in slaves.

People were sold into bondage along much of Africa's Atlantic coast, from Senegal and Gambia southwest to

In this 19th-century illustration, captured Africans are being turned over to slave traders. Notice the man brandishing a stick (center), about to strike a captive, and the person being led away in despair (left). (The Library of Congress)

How the Slave Trade Changed Africa

It was impossible for contact with Europeans to leave African society unchanged. The Portuguese introduced maize and cassava, two New World plants, to Africa in the 1500s. Both crops yield more calories per acre than sorghum or millet, which are native cereal grasses. The Africans traded for European goods, including cloth. European ships also brought plague, virulent strains of smallpox, and syphilis, a disease imported from the Americas.

Today, social scientists want to know more about Europe's influence. How did the slave trade affect African population growth? How did it alter life for those not captured and transported to the New World? Resolving these issues is tricky, because data on Africa's population during the years of the slave trade are sparse. Researchers often can only estimate past totals, but they are reaching some conclusions.

It appears that the population along the west coast of Africa decreased 10 percent to 30 percent between 1760 and 1850. The loss

Angola. Forty percent of the captives may have come from West-central Africa, from the interior of Angola and the Congo River basin. Another important source of slaves was the stretch of territory from the mouth of the Volta River to the Niger River delta. That span of shoreline, which includes coastal areas of Ghana, Togo, Benin, and Nigeria, is known as the Slave Coast, or the Bight of Benin. The Bight of Biafra, the curve in the coastline just south of the Niger delta, yielded many slaves as well. People were also enslaved in Sierra Leone, Senegambia, and the Gold Coast (present-day Ghana). Although the great majority of slaves were of West African and Central African heritage, some came from Mozambique and Madagascar, far to the east, and from the Sudanese grassland east of the Sahara Desert.

occurred unevenly. Senegambia (modern Senegal and Gambia) weathered a small decline, while Angola saw its population ravaged. Travelers in Angola passed through many "empty quarters"—once-populous regions that contained no villages. The people who lived there had been captured or had fled to larger, fortified settlements.

More males than females were taken into slavery in most places, and life changed drastically for the women left behind. Some cleared land and plowed fields, performing jobs that had belonged to men. Many were enslaved by other Africans or shared a husband with another woman. Both slavery and polygamy increased in Africa in the wake of the slave trade and helped restore population levels. Areas that yielded men and women equally to the slave ships, such as eastern Angola and southern Zaire, have few people per square mile even today.

Our image of West Africa in the era of slavery is still emerging, but a key fact is clear. As one researcher stated, "Surely all agree on the remarkable ability of African societies to resist, survive, and adapt in the face of the pressures of slave trade." ◆

People found themselves enslaved for a number of reasons. Most of the slaves who left Africa were prisoners of war. Skirmishes often broke out among the ethnic groups of West Africa. The victors took captives from the ranks of their enemies, and the chiefs traded their prisoners to the Europeans in exchange for colored beads, cloth, guns, whiskey, iron, copper, and other goods. Ethnic warfare alone, however, could not meet the huge demand for slave labor. People who taxed community resources, such as widows, orphans, lawbreakers, and the poor, were also sold into bondage. There were even reports of persons entering slavery voluntarily to escape starvation in times of famine. Finally, slave raiders—both European and African—filtered into the countryside to snatch unsuspecting people from their villages.

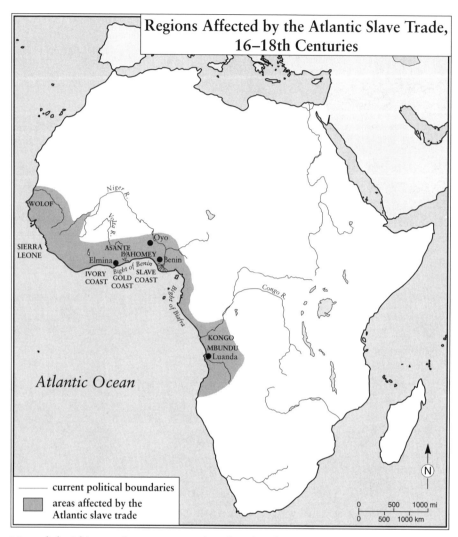

Regions Affected by the Atlantic Slave Trade, 16–18th Centuries

WOLOF

SIERRA LEONE

ASANTE
Elmina DAHOMEY
Oyo
Benin
IVORY COAST GOLD COAST SLAVE COAST
Bight of Benin
Bight of Biafra

Niger R.
Volta R.
Congo R.

KONGO
MBUNDU
Luanda

Atlantic Ocean

N

current political boundaries

areas affected by the Atlantic slave trade

0   500   1000 mi
0   500   1000 km

Most of the Africans who were captured and enslaved came from the West African coastal region that stretches from modern Senegal in the north to Angola in the south.

A Rich African Inheritance

To those who stood to profit from them—the owners of slave ships and the operators of plantations and mines—slaves were a commodity and nothing more. In truth, the people of West Africa were heirs to a rich cultural heritage. The Slave

Coast was their treasure house of music and magic, of stories, drumming, and dance. The Africans' beliefs and customs gave meaning and order to their lives. Although the West Africans were from various ethnic groups, anthropologists say that they were part of a single culture. Their languages, beliefs, and forms of artistic expression were more alike than different.

The West Africans of the slave-trading years left no written record of their history or daily routine. The picture of their life that we have today comes largely from the work of 19th-century travelers and 20th-century social scientists. New findings continue to alter modern understanding of the West African past.

Africa is a continent of old civilizations. Great kingdoms and empires arose in West Africa hundreds of years before Europeans explored the region. Their people built cities such as Luanda, Timbuktu, and Benin, and they made tools and weapons from iron. The first important empire, ancient Ghana, was situated between the Senegal and Niger Rivers in what is now southeastern Mauritania and western Mali. With gold fields directly to its south, ancient Ghana grew rich and powerful. By the 11th century, it controlled trade routes between present-day Morocco and the forests of West Africa.

As historic Ghana declined after 1200, the Empire of Mali emerged. It covered a vast area, from the coastal lands that make up modern Senegal, Gambia, and Guinea-Bissau through most of present-day Mali and into Mauritania and Algeria. Mali's rulers appear to have practiced Islam. Its most enlightened king, Mansa Musa, made a pilgrimage to Mecca in the 1320s and opened diplomatic relations with Tunis and Egypt. He welcomed Islamic scholars and artisans into Mali.

Songhay, once part of ancient Mali, overtook the empire in the 1400s. Songhay, too, had notable leaders, including Askia Muhammad, who assumed the throne in 1493. During his reign, Timbuktu gained renown as a center of Islamic learning. He instituted a sophisticated form of government in which governors supervised provinces within the empire.

Moroccan forces overran the Songhay capital of Gao in 1591, ending the kingdom's prominence. But other empires remained powerful in West Africa throughout the years of the European slave trade. The last great kingdom was the Ashanti Empire, situated largely in modern Ghana. It survived until the start of the 20th century, when it was defeated by Great Britain, which was colonizing the region.

Although many West Africans inhabited cities and towns and worked as artisans, most of the Africans brought to the New World came from farming societies, such as the Mandinka, Yoruba, Ewe, and Igbo peoples. They raised yams, rice, maize, and cassava (a starchy root), and they supplemented their diet by hunting and fishing. Africa was home as well to fishing societies such as the Kru and herders of goats, sheep, and cattle, notably the Fulani and Wolof. These peoples and others contributed greatly to the growth of maritime and livestock-raising enterprises in the New World.

The slaves belonged to a culture that valued fertility. "Without children you are naked," stated a Yoruba proverb. Children ensured that the extended family, or kinship group, would continue. Adults needed the younger generation to care for them in old age and to secure their status as ancestors. Mortality among young children was high. Many succumbed to tropical diseases. Calcium deficiency, due to a shortage of animal milk, hampered some children's growth and development. To help avoid this, mothers commonly breast-fed their children for as long as four years.

The people of West and central Africa spoke many different languages belonging to the Niger-Congo subfamily within the Niger-Kordofanian language family. Languages within a family group originally evolved from a single parent language, but they can vary greatly. They can be as dissimilar as English, Polish, Spanish, and Greek, which are all members of the Indo-European language family. A British slave-ship captain named William Smith commented on the diversity of speech in one small portion of coastal West Africa. "As for the languages of *Gambia,* they are so many and so different," Smith wrote, "that the Natives, on either Side of the River, cannot understand each other. . . ." Africa continues to be a continent of many tongues. Today, more than 200 distinct languages are spoken in Nigeria alone.

Deeply Held Beliefs

Religion governed life in West Africa during the years of the slave trade. Many events, from births to marriages to business transactions, had religious significance. Although a number of people had converted to Islam or Christianity following contact with North Africans or Europeans, most held traditional beliefs. They worshiped a supreme being that was parent to a large assembly of lesser gods. Most African societies believed in a supreme being that was a benevolent father. To some, however, the creator was female; for example, the Igbo people revered an earth mother named Ala.

Many of the minor gods lived in nature. They controlled phenomena such as thunder and lightning, or they dwelled in lakes, rivers, trees, and animals. Other gods had power over human health and fertility.

Gods and people interacted closely. Sometimes a god took possession of a person spiritually, by entering his or her body during a time of religious ecstasy. Sympathetic gods

Every house has its "fetish" hanging up, and every man has a "fetish" charm about his person. There is a devil fetish for driving away evil spirits, and another for bringing good luck.

◆

—Richard Francis Burton,
A Mission to Gelele,
King of Dahome (1864)

might reveal the future to persons skilled in the art of divination. One common way to foretell the future was to cast stones, palm nuts, or cowrie shells on a board and interpret the pattern that they formed. Practitioners of the Yoruba method called *ifa* memorized hundreds of fortune-telling verses, each corresponding to a pattern on the divining board. They recited these verses in response to people's questions.

The West Africans had to appease another group from the spirit world—their departed ancestors. The men and women of bygone generations had founded the villages and kinship groups to which the living now belonged. For that reason, they demanded respect, even in death. It was wise to venerate the ancestors, because they could persuade the gods to grant health and good fortune to their descendants. And ancestors who felt neglected had been known to meddle in people's lives, causing sickness, misfortune, and death.

A ceremony honoring ancestors could be a public event complete with dancing, singing, and drumming. Some members of the large Yoruba and Igbo ethnic groups dressed up in costumes and masks resembling the dead during ritual ancestor worship. In contrast, a person might choose to honor his or her ancestors privately with an offering of food and refreshment.

Olaudah Equiano, an Igbo and one of the first blacks to write a book in English, recalled his mother worshiping at his grandmother's tomb in the 18th century. He wrote, "There she made her libations, and spent most of the night in cries and lamentations. I have often been extremely terrified on these occasions. The loneliness of the place, the darkness of the night, and the ceremony of libation, naturally awful and gloomy, were heightened by my mother's lamentations. . . ."

Because family members gained status after death, funerals were very important. Without a proper burial, the deceased individual would be blocked from entering the spirit realm. The restless, unhappy ghost would wander the world and cause trouble for the living. Funerals were complex, costly, and emotional. An 18th-century witness to a West African funeral described it this way: "They begin with Crying, and at Night they go to Singing and Dancing, and continue so doing till the Time they break up and depart." It was common for family members to decorate a loved one's grave with belongings the person valued in life.

The Yoruba, the Fon, and other West African peoples taught that an ancestor could be reborn in the body of a descendant. In fact, many Yoruba children bore the name Babatunde (Father Returns) or Yetunde (Mother Returns). The reborn ancestor-spirit would chart the child's destiny and then act as a guardian, directing the young person along his or her course in life.

The guardian was only one facet of a complex human soul. The most obvious part of the soul was the conscious human personality. It was able to leave the body during sleep and travel the countryside creating dreams. After death, the personality stood before the supreme being to justify the person's actions in life. Every soul also included a moral guide, or conscience. The West Africans viewed their sense of right and wrong as a sign that the supreme being was present within them. This part of the soul returned to the creator at death. Finally, the soul had a shadow, or dark side, from which all wicked thoughts and impulses came.

The flip side of religious life was a belief in magic. Dark magic lurked in the forests beyond the borders of the village. People had to be wary of witches, who were possessed by evil spirits and had frightening powers.

They also mould images from clay, and bake them. We have seen curious groups of these in some parts of the country. Upon the death of a great man, they make representations of him, sitting in state, with his wives and attendants seated around him.

—Brodie Cruickshank, *Eighteen Years on the Gold Coast of Africa* (1853)

Witches could withhold needed rain, turn people into animals, make themselves invisible, seep through the walls of houses, and cause sores and disease. And because supernatural beings could create illness in humans, people needed charms and amulets to protect themselves. Women commonly strung their charms, or fetishes, onto necklaces. The priests who supplied these powerful objects enjoyed high social status. They knew how to counteract magic, and they acted as healers as well. They had mastered the art of treating illnesses with leaves, bark, roots, and herbs.

Music and Dance

Only a few people studied to be priest-healers, but everyone made music. "The Africans from whom the slaves had descended lived in a world of sound," one historian has written. People sang in the fields as they worked, and they marked nearly every occasion by singing, dancing, and playing instruments. Music marked changes in the growing season, the crowning of kings, and the birth of babies. Music accompanied preparation for hunting or war. African music was remarkable for its complex rhythms. In a typical song, three or more rhythmic patterns might be heard at once, coming from the drums or from the clapping and stamping of the participants.

The West Africans liked to sing in groups. Their songs often followed a style known as "call and response," in which one person called out a phrase, and the others responded as a chorus. Singers felt free to improvise, or to vary the lyrics, tone, or melody of their song.

Dancing was another group activity used to celebrate marriage and birth and to honor the dead. A dance performed in planting season ensured a bountiful crop. The movement of dance was vigorous and athletic. People used their whole bodies, twisting, bending, reaching, and leaping. They tilted their torsos forward, then arched their spines and threw their heads and shoulders back. Like singers, dancers often improvised, because dance was a means of communication. Gestures, mime, costumes, masks, and body decoration all had symbolic importance. People enjoyed dancing outdoors, with the men forming one line and the women forming another. The lines moved toward each other and apart again, in time to music. Sometimes people stood in a circle and clapped their hands as dancers inside the ring leaped and gestured to a rapid drum beat.

Those skilled at playing musical instruments were popular in the community. African musicians played a variety of drums. They fashioned flutes from bamboo, hollow reeds, gourds, and animal horns. They strummed several kinds of stringed instruments, including lutes, zithers, bows, and harps. The *banjil,* also called a *mbanza,* was a stringed instrument made from a gourd or hollow piece of wood. Strands of horse hair or plant fibers formed its strings. A Portuguese visitor to the western coast of Africa in the years of exploration admired the region's skillful lute players. "They express their thoughts and make themselves understood so clearly that almost anything that can be said with words they can render with their fingers by touching this instrument," he wrote.

Telling Tales

Storytellers always drew a crowd, too. The West Africans had no written literature, so they passed along tales through the oral tradition. Oral historians known as *griots* recited epic tales of early empires, great battles, and wise leaders and teachers. They kept alive the knowledge of a revered African past. The West Africans repeated proverbs and riddles to teach proper social conduct, and they recounted myths and legends to explain the origins of their ethnic groups. Because they lived so close to nature, they often told stories about animals. The trickster was a favorite character. It took the form of a wily tortoise throughout much of West Africa, of the spider Anansi among the Akan speakers in what is now Ghana, and of a rabbit in East Africa.

The story "Why the Hare Runs Away," about a hare that steals water from the other animals, was a favorite among the Ewe people. In the story, the animals set a trap for the mischievous hare, hoping to get even. They make an image of a person and cover it with sticky birdlime. The scheme works. The hare gets angry when the figure makes no response to his greeting. When he slaps it, his paw gets stuck in the birdlime. Making up stories about animals with human traits was a way for people to understand themselves and their place in the world.

Carving and Casting

When the West Africans made art with their hands, it tended to be three-dimensional. Their sculpture, whether of wood, stone, or bronze, depicted the gods, animals, and human life. Artists did not try to create realistic images. Instead, they distorted features for effect. Because society placed such importance on fertility, sculptors often exaggerated the genitals and breasts on their carvings.

Some sculptors displayed a level of expertise rare in any culture. Yoruban artists were unusually skilled in casting their statues in bronze. In the 11th and 12th centuries they created a series of life-size heads that are admired throughout the world today. The original purpose of the heads has been forgotten, but art historians think they might have represented dead rulers and been used on ceremonial occasions.

A coiled snake adorns a terra-cotta pot made during the years of the slave trade in what is now Ghana. (Photograph by Franko Khoury. National Museum of African Art, Eliot Elisofon Photographic Archives, Smithsonian Institution)

Artists in the royal city of Benin (not to be confused with the neighboring country Benin) made brass figures at the time of the slave trade that are famed for their beauty and technical sophistication.

West African artisans also made terra-cotta pottery. Blacksmiths forged agricultural tools and decorative items, and women wove baskets and cloth.

Africans Uprooted

The people captured and sold into slavery lost their place in this vibrant culture. They were torn from their families, their homes, and their life's work. They were marched overland to the coast with ropes around their necks, branded like livestock, and kept in crowded pens until it was time to sail. Conditions were so poor that many died of illness or hardship before boarding a slave vessel. Those who survived appeared to take nothing with them, yet they carried much that was precious in their minds and hearts.

NOTES

p. 1 "the spot of earthly paradise." Quoted in Daniel J. Boorstin, *The Discoverers* (New York: Random House, 1983), p. 242.

p. 2 "These pioneers found Africa . . ." Benjamin Quarles, *The Negro in the Making of America* (New York: Simon & Schuster, 1987), p. 26.

p. 4 "have bought this year . . ." Quoted in Richard S. Dunn, *Sugar and Slaves* (London: Jonathan Cape, 1973), p. 68.

p. 5 "For though their bodies were . . ." Gomes Eannes de Zurara, *The Chronicle of the Discovery and Conquest of Guinea*, vol. 100, Charles R. Beazley and Edgar Prestage, trans. (London: Hakluy & Society, 1899), pp. 84–85.

p. 7 "Surely all agree . . ." Patrick Manning, "Local Versus Regional Impact of Slave Exports on Africa," in Dennis D. Cordell and Joel W. Gregory, eds., *African Population and Capitalism: Historical Perspectives* (Boulder, Colo.: Westview Press, 1987), p. 37.

p. 10 "Without children you are naked." Quoted in John Iliffe, *Africans: The History of a Continent* (Cambridge: Cambridge University Press, 1995), p. 68.

p. 11 "As for the languages . . ." Quoted in J. L. Dillard, *Black English: Its History and Usage in the United States* (New York: Random House, 1972), p. 73.

p. 11 "Every house has its 'fetish' . . ." Richard Francis Burton, *A Mission to Gelele, King of Dahome,* vol. 2 (London: Tinsley Brothers, 1864), p. 361.

p. 12 "There she made her libations . . ." Olaudah Equiano, *The Interesting Narrative of the Life of* Olaudah Equiano, *or* Gustavus Vassa, *the African. Written by Himself.* London, 1794. Reprinted in Vincent Carretta, ed., *Unchained Voices* (Lexington, Ky.: The University Press of Kentucky, 1996), p. 193.

p. 13 "They begin with Crying . . ." Francis Moore, *Travels Into the Inland Parts of Africa* (London: Edward Crane, 1738), p. 130.

p. 13 "They also mould images . . ." Brodie Cruickshank, *Eighteen Years on the Gold Coast of Africa* (London: Hurst and Blackett, 1853), p. 270.

p. 14 "The Africans from whom . . ." Lawrence W. Levine, "African Culture and Slavery in the United States," in Joseph Harris, ed., *Global Dimensions of the African Diaspora* (2d ed., Washington, D.C.: Howard University Press, 1993), p. 102.

p. 15 "They express their thoughts . . ." Quoted in Georges Balandier, *Daily Life in the Kingdom of the Kongo from the Sixteenth to the Eighteenth Century* (New York: Pantheon Books, 1968), p. 232.

2

First Encounters

Africans Adapt to the New World

The trip across the Atlantic
Ocean was a voyage of terror and hardship for the enslaved
African people. Many had never seen a European before and
feared their pale-skinned captors. They asked themselves,
Who were these white men? Did they inhabit the sea, or had
they come from the land of the dead? Were their black shoes
made from Africans' skin? And those red flags they flew
—had they been dyed with Africans' blood?

A sailor on an English vessel described the captives' terror
at the start of their journey. He wrote in his diary, "The slaves
all night in a turmoil. They felt the ship's movement. A worse
howling I never did hear, like the poor mad souls in Bedlam
Hospital. The men shook their fetters which was deafening."

A Nightmarish Journey

Shackled in pairs, sometimes with chains around their necks, the prisoners were confined in the dark, filthy space between decks. With no more than five feet of headroom and less than half a square yard of floor space per person, it was impossible to stand erect or move about freely. Human beings lay atop one another in some ships, stacked like lifeless bundles of cargo.

The slave merchants packed as many people as possible into their ships to offset losses from deaths. Death was so common during the ocean crossing that the Portuguese word for slave ship was *tumba,* meaning "coffin." A voyage across the Atlantic might take three months in the late 17th century. The captain of a slave ship could expect to lose one-fourth of his slaves and crew during the trip. In rare cases, nearly half of those aboard perished. The 1716 voyage of the *Indian Queen* was one such devastating journey. By the time this

Crews used whips and firearms to maintain control in the holds of slave ships. (The Library of Congress)

British ship docked in Buenos Aires in South America, 140 of the approximately 300 people it carried had died from smallpox, and another 88 were ill.

Smallpox, measles, and other contagious diseases spread rapidly in the packed quarters and claimed numerous lives. Many people succumbed to dysentery, or "bloody flux," after eating contaminated food. Desperate captives attempted suicide, either by starving themselves or by jumping overboard with their partners in chains. They hoped to be reborn in Africa in the bodies of their descendants. Not every slave who drowned was a suicide, however. At times crew members threw sick people overboard to prevent the transmission of disease. There were reports of sharks following slave ships for a month or longer.

The traders took some steps to protect the slaves' health. Crew members brought the captives up on deck periodically to get exercise and fresh air. Many traders fed the enslaved Africans familiar foods, such as rice and yams, although supplies could run out on long voyages. In the 18th century, European countries passed laws limiting the number of persons a ship could carry. England, for example, allowed five enslaved Africans for every three tons of a ship's weight. Whether those laws were strictly obeyed, though, is doubtful.

Worse than crowding for many slaves and more trying than hunger or disease was thirst. A ship's water supply had to last through the voyage, so it was strictly rationed. There was never enough water, especially when illness and perspiration increased the demand. Sometimes mosquitoes or algae contaminated barrels of water and made them unfit for drinking. Scholars now believe that dehydration killed as many captives as did disease.

The building of faster ships in the 1700s did more to lower the death rate than anything else. By 1730, about 15 percent of slaves and crew members died before reaching port, compared to 25 percent in the 1600s. A century later, the rate had fallen below 10 percent.

The terrifying voyage from Africa to the New World was called the Middle Passage. It was the second stretch of a three-part, or triangular, trade route. Ships left European ports laden with the products of factories and mills. They docked along the African coast, completing the first leg of the triangle. There the officers traded their cargo for captives. From Africa, the ships sailed for the New World, where planters awaited a fresh supply of enslaved workers.

> I *became so sick and low that I was not able to eat, nor had I the least desire to taste any thing. I now wished for the last friend, Death, to relieve me.*
>
>
>
> —Olaudah Equiano, recalling the Middle Passage in his life narrative (1794)

After delivering the parched, malnourished survivors of the Middle Passage, the crews loaded their ships with barrels of rum, bales of cotton and tobacco, rice, sugar, indigo, and ginger. The venture known as triangle trade ended where it began, as the ships carried the bounty of the colonies back to their home ports.

The Origin of a New Culture

African-American culture was born during the Middle Passage, when people found themselves separated from their friends and shackled to strangers from different African nations. The slave traders deliberately mixed people up to reduce the risk of mutiny. Without a common language, the prisoners would be less likely to organize and fight against their captors, the slave merchants believed. The English captain William Smith reasoned that by "having some of every Sort on board, there will be no more Likelihood of their succeeding in a Plot, than of finishing the Tower of Babel."

The possibility of a slave uprising was very real. In 1721, a man from Sierra Leone named Tomba led several other slaves in an attack on their ship's crew. The captain's men apprehended the rebels and executed two of them. Other slave mutinies were more successful. In 1839, slaves seized control of a Spanish ship, the *Amistad,* in the waters off Cuba. They attempted to sail toward Africa, but they were detained by American authorities off Long Island, New York. In a legal battle that gripped the nation, they won the right to return to Africa in U.S. federal court.

Women masterminded the takeover of the *Thomas,* an English slave ship, in 1797. Using weapons stolen from an unguarded chest, the enslaved people murdered most of the crew and seized control of the ship. They were returning to Africa when a British naval vessel, H.M. Frigate *Thames,* caught up with the *Thomas* and captured it.

The Africans crossing the ocean may not have understood one another at first, but they soon found ways to communicate. They picked up phrases from the languages of their captors, and they learned words from one another's tongues. In addition to seeing themselves as members of a particular ethnic group, they began to view themselves as part of a larger community, the population of enslaved Africans.

A friendship made during the Middle Passage might endure for decades. When an enslaved person called someone "shipmate" in Jamaica, it meant that he or she was a fellow survivor of the horrific journey and as close as a brother or sister. The strong tie extended to the shipmate's relatives as well. Children commonly called a parent's shipmate "uncle" or "aunt." In the Dutch colony of Surinam, the word for a shipmate was *sibi.* Today people living

> The deck, that is the floor of their rooms, was so covered with the blood and mucous which had proceeded from them in consequence of the flux, that it resembled a slaughter-house. It is not in the power of the human imagination to picture to itself a situation more dreadful or disgusting.
>
> ◆
>
> —Alexander Falconbridge, *An Account of the Slave Trade* (1788)

there use that word to describe a close friend or someone with whom they have shared an adventure.

First Views of a White World

A shipmate seemed like an old friend after those terrible weeks at sea. It was comforting to have this familiar figure close at hand when stepping ashore in a strange white world. For although the Europeans were newcomers to a particular colony as well, they had made the place their own. They all came from the same country in Europe and spoke a single language, while the Africans represented diverse societies.

> The Negroes in general are strongly attached to their countrymen, but above all to such of their companions as came in the same ship with them from Africa. . . . the term shipmate is understood among them as signifying a relationship of the most endearing nature.
>
> ◆
>
> —Bryan Edwards, *History of the British Colonies in the West Indies* (1793)

In colonies such as Barbados, the Africans saw white men and women riding about on horses and living in two-story brick houses. These people belonged to the wealthy planter class. Other European immigrants lived more modestly. They had come as indentured servants, agreeing to work without pay for an extended period, usually four or seven years, in exchange for their passage to the New World. At the end of that period, they were free to live wherever they chose and to seek whatever paid employment they could find.

The number of indentured servants declined sharply once the planters discovered the advantages of owning slaves. Enslaved workers complained less than indentured servants did about tropical food and insects. The planters spent less to feed and clothe their slaves than they spent on servants of their own race. Approximately 500,000 indentured servants sailed for the New World from one port, Bristol, England, in the 1660s. Two decades later, the situation was far different. A mere 601 indentured servants embarked at Bristol between 1680 and 1686.

For most of the Africans arriving in the Americas, life was short and hard. They were herded into a slave market, sold to the highest bidder, and worked to death. Slave owners found that it was cheaper to replace dead slaves with new ones from Africa than to treat existing workers well and keep them healthy. The labor was most grueling on the sugar plantations of the British West Indies, where even the hardiest slave could expect to survive only three years.

Europe had a sweet tooth that never seemed satisfied and a strong thirst for rum, the liquor distilled from sugar cane. The island colonies produced a variety of crops, but it was the sugar industry that demanded the most slaves and determined where they were sent.

Punishing Work on the Sugar Plantations

From morning until night, sugar-plantation slaves dug furrows, planted cuttings, fertilized the growing crops, and slashed away old stands of sugar cane. At harvest time, they used machetes to cut through hundreds of mature canes, each one more than an inch thick. If someone collapsed from exhaustion, an overseer was at hand to give that person a beating.

Brutal punishment was part of daily life. Enslaved Africans in Barbados received 50 lashes with a whip for walking beyond the plantation boundaries on Sunday, their one day free from work. More serious offenses earned them branding, which, as one observer noted, made them "shriek with despair."

The furnaces that processed raw cane into sugar crystals burned 24 hours a day. Slaves continually fed crushed cane

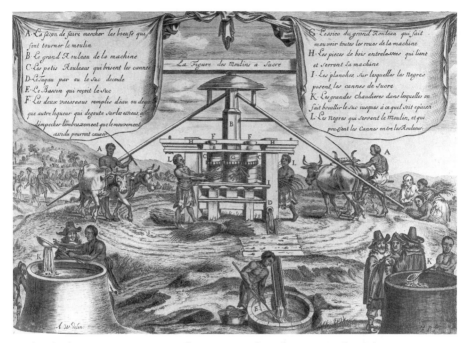

Enslaved Africans operate a sugar mill on a West Indian plantation in the 17th century. Juice from the pressed sugar cane flows into a cistern (bottom center). It is boiled to form a syrup in copper cauldrons (bottom left and right). (The Library Company of Philadelphia)

into the furnaces, taking only a four-hour break for sleep. A person who died was pushed out of the way so that others might carry on the work.

Though abused, overworked, and poorly clothed and fed, the immigrant Africans tried to feel at home in the New World. They built thatched huts in circular groupings that resembled the villages of their homeland. A visitor to Martinique in the late 17th century saw slave huts with round, pointed roofs like those built in Africa by the Mandinka people. The enslaved people gave their children African names: Mingo, Cuffee, Quasha, Affrah. They acquainted themselves with the plants and animals that thrived on the western shores of the Atlantic. The farmers among them studied the climate and soil. The people would retain what they could of African life while adapting in order to survive.

The Maroons of Jamaica _____

Every colony with swamps, mountains, or other rough terrain sheltered communities of runaway slaves. Known as maroons, a name
derived from the Spanish word *cimarrón* (stray cattle), these groups
challenged the authority of every slaveholding nation. There were maroons in Surinam, Brazil, Haiti, Mexico, and even the United States. One
of the largest maroon populations lived in Jamaica.

In 1655, England seized Jamaica from Spain. Most Spanish plantation
owners fled the island, leaving 1,500 enslaved laborers behind. Wasting
no time, the slaves headed for the island's mountainous, tree-covered
interior. To the extent that it was possible, they re-created their African
way of life. They preserved words, proverbs, and beliefs, and they raised
yams, squash, and other crops. The few Spaniards who had stayed
behind lived in the hills as well. Together, the maroons and the Spaniards created havoc by stealing British provisions and harassing the new
settlers. The British coaxed some maroons into signing treaties, but
these had little effect.

By 1720, the maroons lived in two main groups, the Leeward Maroons
and the Windward Maroons, and they had become a powerful force in
Jamaica. They were too strong, the white population complained. Their

Connecting with Words

One of the first challenges faced by whites and Africans in
the New World was communication. The Europeans knew
nothing of the Africans' languages, and the Africans had
trouble understanding one another. Although the slaves had
picked up a few words from their captors and shipmates,
they were largely ignorant of any language but their own.

Pidgins developed quickly in the plantation colonies. A
pidgin is a simplified language used among speakers of
different languages. It employs words from two or more

raids disrupted island life, and their presence inspired current slaves to escape. Britain decided to resolve the maroon problem through warfare.

England may have had trained soldiers and better weapons, but the maroons had mastered the landscape. The terrain was far different from what they had known in Africa, yet they moved swiftly through trees and over mountains. They had dynamic leaders who inspired them to fight —leaders like Nanny, the female warrior and priest-healer of the Windward Maroons, who is a Jamaican national hero today.

Nanny's fearlessness was so renowned that she became the subject of legends. She was rumored to catch British cannonballs with her buttocks. Soldiers were warned that she kept a cauldron of water that boiled without a flame and had the power to lure them to their deaths.

The maroons fought for years, but by 1739, they were running out of provisions. Cudjoe, leader of the Leeward Maroons, entered into a treaty with the British. Nanny's followers reluctantly consented to a treaty three months later. In return for the right to self-governance, the maroons agreed to hunt down runaway slaves and return them to their owners.

Some maroons complied with these treaties and later ones, but others continued to fight. In 1800, 58 years after Nanny's death, Britain shipped the most rebellious Jamaican maroons to Nova Scotia. Those who survived a winter of hard labor set sail for Sierra Leone with the aid of British abolitionists.

standard languages within an elementary grammatical framework, allowing different cultural groups to conduct business and communicate easily. English pidgins dispense with irregular verbs, while French pidgins lack the separate masculine and feminine adjectives employed in standard French. Pidgins have been used at various times in U.S. history, as when Native Americans and immigrant Chinese workers needed to communicate with the English-speaking population.

Slaves working as house servants and mechanics were in frequent contact with the white population and soon learned their language. Plantation workers, in contrast, seldom spoke with their white owners. They relied on the regional pidgin, retaining their African languages for secret talks in their quarters. Newly enslaved people arriving from Africa kept the linguistic ties to the homeland alive.

New Beliefs and Old Ones

Just as the Portuguese baptized large numbers of slaves, other slaveholding nations imposed their beliefs on the Africans under their control. For instance, Haiti's Code Noir of 1685, which was a group of laws governing the ownership of slaves, required that every slave in this French colony receive instruction and baptism in the Roman Catholic faith.

The early planters of the British colonies, in contrast, made no effort to convert their slaves, believing that Britain had outlawed the enslavement of Christians. But starting in 1701, missionaries from the Church of England taught that slavery was part of the Christian social order. They quoted the Bible (Eph. 6:5) as proof: "Slaves be obedient to your masters." Thus, a slave could now be converted to Christianity and remain in bondage.

Despite efforts at conversion, African religions thrived —away from the eyes of most whites—in Haiti, Barbados, and elsewhere. A French priest in Haiti observed in 1712 that "The Negroes . . . secretly preserve all the superstition of their ancient idolatrous cult alongside the ceremonies of Christianity." African newcomers refreshed the slaves' memories of rituals from home. They sang the songs and repeated the tales of Africa.

In some places, the enslaved population openly celebrated its African heritage. The slave-turned-writer Olaudah Equiano noted, "When I came to Kingston [Jamaica], I was surprised to see the number of Africans, who were assembled together on Sundays; particularly at a large commodious

Slaves carry water from a fountain in 19th-century colonial Brazil. (The Library of Congress)

place called Spring Path. Here each different nation of Africa meet and dance, after the manner of their own country."

Then, gradually, the flood of immigration slowed. The United States banned the importation of slaves in 1808. Great Britain had resolved to end its slave trade in 1807, and in 1833, Britain abolished slavery throughout its empire. By 1836, both Spain and Portugal had formally outlawed the slave trade. Nevertheless, the transport of slaves continued illegally for more than 30 years, with more than 600,000 slaves entering Cuba, a Spanish colony, between 1811 and 1870. More than 1 million came to Brazil in the same period.

The end of the slave trade broke the connection with Africa for the inhabitants of many regions. Cut off from their homelands, living in isolated groups on plantations, the enslaved people devised ways to make life meaningful. They took wives and husbands, although the laws did not recognize slave marriages. They formed households and kinship groups, even if loved ones might be sold at any time. The people created rituals for burying their dead, welcoming newborns, and treating the sick. They united in prayer as a refuge from mistreatment.

As new generations were born on American soil and the memory of Africa dimmed, African names gave way to European nicknames. Customs and beliefs evolved that were both African and American, a blend of the old and the new. In spite of slavery, life went on.

NOTES

p. 20   "The slaves all night . . ." Quoted in W. McGowan, "African Resistance to the Atlantic Slave Trade in West Africa," *Slavery and Abolition* (May 1990), p. 20.

p. 23   "I became so sick . . ." Equiano, p. 203.

p. 23   "having some of every Sort . . ." Quoted in Dillard, p. 74.

p. 24   "The deck, that is the floor . . ." Quoted in James Pope-Hennessy, *Sins of the Fathers: A Study of the Atlantic Slave Traders, 1441–1807* (London: Weidenfeld and Nicolson, 1967), p. 102.

p. 25   "The Negroes in general . . ." Quoted in Pope-Hennessy, p. 103.

p. 26   "shriek with despair." Quoted in Dunn, p. 241.

p. 30   "The Negroes . . . secretly preserve . . ." Quoted in Albert J. Raboteau, *Slave Religion: The "Invisible Institution" in the Antebellum South* (Oxford: Oxford University Press, 1978), p. 25.

p. 30   "When I came to Kingston . . ." Equiano, in Carretta, p. 257.

3

"I Shall Not Live Here Always!"

Slave Culture in the United States

The first Africans in British North America arrived in 1619. They were 20 in number and came on a Dutch vessel that docked in Jamestown, Virginia. For a long time, the number of blacks in the 13 colonies remained small. In 1650, for example, blacks accounted for only 4 percent of the population. The white colonists treated those Africans as indentured servants and granted them freedom after four years' labor.

In the 18th century, new laws limited the rights of African workers in the British colonies. Those laws banned interracial marriages and outlined punishments for worker disobedience. Most ominously, they restricted manumission, or the granting of freedom to black servants. Thus, they created a legal basis for slavery.

The number of Africans in British North America rose rapidly once slavery was established. By the time of the American Revolution, more than one-fifth of the colonial population was black, and most in that group were enslaved. Although slavery was permitted throughout the colonies, most enslaved persons lived in the South, where the warm climate supported plantation farming. A worker's place of origin often determined where he or she was sent. South Carolina planters, for example, preferred slaves from Senegambia and the Sierra Leone region, because they were skilled in growing rice, which became South Carolina's principal export by 1750. Most Europeans were unfamiliar with rice cultivation, and it is unlikely that they could have produced a crop without African expertise.

Slave Labor in the South

Vermont abolished slavery in 1777. By 1804, all of the Northern states had begun the gradual emancipation of their slaves. Slavery in the United States became strictly a southern institution.

Large plantations needed blacksmiths, carpenters, cobblers, and weavers, and slaves performed these jobs. Some southern slaves worked in factories or as domestic servants. Others were skilled artisans who built the mansions of Charleston, South Carolina, and other cities. But most enslaved workers were field hands. They awoke in the dark hours of early morning to be on the job before sunrise. They labored 16 hours a day during the growing season and even longer at harvest time.

Every enslaved African had tasks to perform, regardless of age. Children weeded flower beds or fanned their perspiring masters. Aging women cooked and minded babies, and old men looked after livestock or tended gardens.

While 200 enslaved laborers might live on a Caribbean sugar farm, a typical plantation in the southern United States housed 20 slaves. Most southern farmers raised cotton, especially after 1793, when Eli Whitney invented the cotton gin. Whitney's machine cleaned cotton quickly and efficiently, making it a highly profitable crop to grow. By the middle of the 19th century, cotton accounted for more than half of U.S. exports, bringing in $190 million per year from European markets. The majority of enslaved African Americans, therefore, toiled in cotton fields. They planted and weeded in spring and picked the ripe cotton bolls at summer's end. They ginned the cotton to remove seeds and debris, and they packed it for shipment overseas.

A Valued Commodity

The end of slave importation meant better treatment for enslaved workers throughout the Western Hemisphere. With the supply from Africa dwindling, slave prices rose. Farmers protected their investment by providing better food and easing working conditions. "Negroes are too high in proportion to the price of cotton, and it behooves those who own them to make them last as long as possible," a southern planter concluded in 1849. Life improved more for enslaved people in the United States than for those in other places, thanks to pressure from the abolitionists. These antislavery activists kept constant watch over southern slave owners and publicized any abuse that came to their attention.

Still, conditions remained harsh for enslaved Americans. Beatings, hunger, overwork, and early death were facts of their existence. Laws on southern statute books restricted their activities, due to fears of an uprising. Wary masters suspected that angry slaves might poison them one day or set fire to their homes or cotton harvests.

There were laws against African healing rites, which appeared strange and threatening to whites. Drumming, which accompanied song, dance, and worship in African cultures, was forbidden in some places, too, in the belief that slaves might communicate via their drums and organize a revolt. Georgia's slave code prohibited enslaved people "from using and carrying mischievous and dangerous weapons, or using and keeping drums, horns, or other loud instruments, which may call together or give sign or notice to one another of their wicked designs and intentions. . . ."

Some of these strict laws resulted from Nat Turner's 1831 revolt, a slave rebellion that unnerved whites throughout the South. Turner and five followers killed their master and his family. Joined by more than 60 slaves from nearby plantations in Southampton County, Virginia, they set out for the county seat. They planned to take over an armory, and they murdered 57 whites along the way. Turner was caught six weeks later, and he and 15 of his followers were hanged. An unknown number of blacks died at the hands of lynch mobs.

A few governments were less motivated by fear and more lenient in regulating slaves' actions. For example, the city of New Orleans, Louisiana, set aside times and places for its enslaved residents to congregate. "The slaves have Sunday for a day of recreation, and upon many plantations they dance for several hours during the afternoon," wrote an English tourist in the 19th century. The writer described a joyful, musical scene that he witnessed: "The general movement is what they call the Congo dance; but their music often consists of nothing more than an excavated piece of wood . . . one end of which is a piece of parchment which covers the hollow part on which they beat; this, and the singing or vociferation of those who are dancing, and of those who surround the dancers constitute the whole of their harmony."

Gatherings such as this one were cultural exchanges, opportunities to reminisce about Africa and share innovations. Communication was vital to the culture that was evolving in slave villages and among families. It was a culture thriving under the masters' domination, yet apart from them.

New Generations

Children born in the slave quarters had no memory of Africa. The offspring of New World slaves spoke to one another in the local pidgin. They saw little need for the African languages of their parents.

Once a pidgin has native speakers, linguists refer to it as a *creole* language. Numerous creoles have been spoken by populations of African descent in North America, South America, and the Caribbean. Some fell into disuse through a process called decreolization. Over a few generations, these creoles became more like the languages of the white population. In this way the creoles of most slaves in the United States moved closer to English.

Music in Slave Life

Music, so vital to life in West Africa, remained important for African Americans. Enslaved and free blacks in the United States built instruments like those played in their old lands, such as stringed banjos and the drums observed in 19th-century New Orleans. They also learned to play European instruments, including the violin, guitar, clarinet, and tambourine. Masters often called upon the musicians among their slaves to entertain at parties for whites.

The white people danced so differently from African Americans. The whites held their bodies erect, in the European fashion, and followed repetitive step patterns. They

A white plantation family mingles with enslaved workers on Christmas Eve. The musicians (right) play a banjo and a violin, the former, of African origin, the latter, European. (The Library of Congress)

danced with partners, standing at assigned positions on the floor. There was no improvising, no leaping or reaching.

When given a rare holiday from work, the enslaved people sang and danced in their own way, if permitted. They also sang as they labored in the fields:

> Way down in the bottom—whah the cotton boll's a rotten
> Won't get my hundud all day.

The slaves wove strands of African melodies, Protestant hymns, and bits of Bible stories gleaned from white preachers to fashion a new kind of song: the spiritual.

The mournful spirituals, with their distinctive flat notes that sounded off-key to white ears, often conveyed a hidden message. Spirituals such as "Steal Away, Steal Away," contained veiled instructions for escape. Frederick Douglass, a runaway slave who gained fame as a speaker and writer, recalled another spiritual that had a double meaning. He wrote,

> A keen observer might have detected in our repeated singing of
>> O Canaan, sweet Canaan,
>> I am bound for the land of Canaan,
> something more than a hope of reaching heaven. We meant to reach the *North,* and the North was our Canaan.

The Solace of Religion

Spirituals, of course, were first and foremost songs of faith. Many slaves found comfort and familiarity in the beliefs of their masters. Praying to the whites' God, Jehovah, was not too different from worshiping the supreme being in Africa. The numerous Christian saints resembled the spirits of nature. Although many slaves held on to their traditional religions, thousands converted to Christianity. Most converts were swayed by the preaching of Baptist and Methodist missionaries. In Maryland and Louisiana, states with large Roman Catholic populations, slaves and free blacks who accepted Christianity tended to be baptized as Catholics.

The Baptists and Methodists licensed African Americans to preach.

> I *know moon-rise, I know star-rise,*
>> *Lay dis body down.*
> *I walk in de moonlight, I walk in de starlight,*
>> *To lay dis body down.*
> *I'll walk in de graveyard, I'll walk through de graveyard,*
>> *To lay dis body down.*
> *I'll lie in de grave and stretch out my arms;*
>> *Lay dis body down.*
> *I go to de Judgment in de evenin' ob de day*
>> *When I lay dis body down.*
> *And my soul and your soul will meet in de day*
>> *When I lay dis body down.*
>
> ◆
>
> —A spiritual recorded by Thomas Wentworth Higginson in *Army Life in a Black Regiment* (1869)

Some of these black clergymen started congregations of their own. One of the earliest, the First African Baptist Church, was founded in Savannah, Georgia, in 1788. Other black ministers traveled throughout the South, preaching to their people on plantations and in towns.

African-American ministers retold Bible stories in a way that had a personal meaning for their enslaved congregations. For example, the preachers compared the slaves to the Israelites held captive in Egypt thousands of years earlier. In the Bible's account of the Exodus, in which Moses led the Israelites to freedom, the faithful saw a promise that their slavery would one day end. The United States, like Egypt, would be judged by God and punished.

African Americans interacted closely with God in their churches, just as their forebears had done in Africa. They sang out, "Mass [Master] Jesus is my bosom friend." In dance, they reenacted biblical scenes, such as Joshua's victory

Slave Church on a Cotton Plantation in Tennessee, *a watercolor by Franz Holzlhuber* (Glenbow Collection, Calgary, Alberta, Canada)

at Jericho; they became, for a time, the children of Israel leaving Egypt.

"The way in which we worshiped was almost indescribable," stated a black plantation preacher. "The singing was accompanied by a certain ecstasy of motion, clapping of hands, tossing of heads, which would continue without cessation about half an hour. . . . The old house partook of the ecstasy; it rang with their jubilant shouts, and shook in all its joints." To the white population, such emotional worship was "ungodly."

Many slaves, however, attended church under white supervision. They heard white ministers teach that by obeying their masters, the slaves followed God's will. God wanted them to be docile, to "turn the other cheek" when punished or abused, the preachers said. They taught that slaves had been put on earth only to raise crops.

Any thinking person doubted the truth of such sermons. And so these enslaved workers looked forward to secret prayer meetings in their quarters or in "hush harbors," usually located beside swamps or in the brush. There the slaves felt free to pray as they wished. Peter Randolph, a slave freed in 1847, recalled his joy at these secret prayer meetings. "The slave forgets all his sufferings," Randolph said, "except to remind others of the trials during the past week, exclaiming, 'Thank God, I shall not live here always!'"

African Rites Remembered

There is evidence that traditional beliefs thrived, even among those who adopted Christianity. In the 1990s, an archaeological dig beneath an 18th-century house in Alexandria, Virginia, uncovered small collections of white buttons and broken glass and dishes. Previous owners of the house had kept a number of slaves over the years, and researchers think

In places such as Sapelo, Georgia, the custom of placing objects on loved ones' graves continued into the 20th century. This photograph was taken around 1920.
(Courtesy, Georgia Department of Archives and History)

that the items found were used to foretell the future. The broken bits resemble shards found at ancestral shrines in West Africa. The buttons may have replaced cowrie shells as divination tools.

Gladys-Marie Fry, a professor at the University of Maryland who studied the findings, pointed out that enslaved people never knew when they might be sold, beaten, or raped. "The belief in divination offered a strong means of coping with such enormous brutality," she said.

The slaves' burial customs also reflected their African roots. Funerals took place as long as a month after interment, giving souls ample time to reach heaven. A funeral celebrated the fact that the soul was in its new home. African Americans decorated their loved ones' graves with treasured belongings, sea shells, bits of brightly colored glass, carved wooden figures, and even patchwork quilts.

Enslaved men and women taught their children to honor their ancestors and warned that the slighting of an ancestor invited trouble. Parents whispered about witches who moved among ordinary mortals, took animal form, and rode on humans at night. People protected themselves with charms, sometimes called "hands," and lucky horseshoes, and they suspended bottles of salt and pepper over their cabin doors. Those seasonings, they believed, would burn a witch's skin.

Because of the need for charms and cures, the priest-healer remained a high-ranking member of society. "He early appeared on the plantation," wrote the scholar W. E. B. Du Bois in 1900, "and found his function as the healer of the sick, the interpreter of the unknown, the comforter of the sorrowing, the supernatural avenger of the wrong and the one who rudely, but picturesquely, expressed the longing, disappointment and resentment of a stolen and oppressed people." Priest-healers were called root doctors in some places, due to their knowledge of herbal medicine. They were also known

An enslaved woman and child on Drayton's Plantation, Hilton Head, South Carolina, when it was occupied by Union troops during the Civil War. The woman wears an African-style fetish necklace. (New Hampshire Historical Society F3804)

Slaves and Indians _____

A fricans in the New World encountered not just whites but indige-
nous peoples as well. The native people of the West Indies were all
but extinct when the first enslaved Africans arrived there, but many
Indians survived in places such as Brazil and North America. Blacks and
Indians were united by their distrust of whites. In the United States, from
the colonial period through the Civil War, Native Americans sheltered
runaway slaves, and the two groups often intermarried.

Slaves found husbands and wives among the Creek, the Cherokee,
and other peoples of the South. Blacks also mixed with the Shinnecock
Indians of Long Island, the Narraganset of Rhode Island, and other
northern ethnic groups. Contact with the black population affected
Indians' relations with the U.S. government, and it also altered Indian
culture.

The number of marriages that took place between blacks and Indians
cannot be determined because the native people kept no written records. However, accounts by 18th- and 19th-century observers often
mention the presence of African Americans in Indian communities.
Thomas Jefferson, describing the few surviving Indians in Virginia, wrote
in 1800, "there remain of the Mattoponies three or four men only, and
they have more Negro than Indian blood in them." An 1834 census of the
Choctaw people described a number of individuals as "half Indian and
half Negro."

as hoodoo doctors, two-facers, and wangateurs. They could
be recognized by the crooked canes they often carried and
by their "conjure bags" filled with charms and potions.

Folk Tales in the New World

Very few slaves were taught to read and write, so they
maintained their oral traditions. They told and retold tales

Evidence of black and Indian mixing can also be found in newspaper advertisements placed by the owners of runaway slaves. One owner described his missing slave as "half Negro and half Indian . . . He plays the fiddle, and speaks good English and his country Indian." Another escapee "Was born of an Indian woman, and looks much like an Indian. . . ."

In southern Florida, many people fleeing slavery found a refuge among the Seminole Indians. Seminole lands encompassed the Everglades, a vast, swampy, subtropical wilderness that offered many hiding places. After the United States acquired Florida from Spain in 1819, the government began a campaign to remove the Seminole and open the territory to white settlement. The Seminole fought fiercely against U.S. forces to protect their homes and their families. According to law, any child born to an enslaved mother was also a slave. The Seminole men feared that the children of slave women they had married would be captured and sold into slavery.

Research demonstrates that African Americans influenced the cultures of native populations that they joined. Their impact is most evident in Native American folk tales. A number of Indian peoples have passed down stories that strongly resemble popular African folk tales. For example, the Cherokee like to tell a story about an opossum and a terrapin picking persimmons. While the opossum is in a tree tossing fruit down to his friend, a hungry wolf turns up. The quick-thinking opossum throws a persimmon into the wolf's mouth and chokes him. In the analogous African story, a trickster drops a stone down a greedy foe's throat.

similar to the ones their ancestors had enjoyed in Africa. Animals still tricked one another and succeeded by their wits in these stories, but the lion and monkey were now joined by the bear, the opossum, and other American creatures.

Researchers and writers such as Joel Chandler Harris and Zora Neale Hurston have recorded hundreds of African-American folk tales. Many are strongly similar to African stories. One of the best-known African-American tales, "The Tar Baby," is a variation of the Ewe story "Why the Hare

Runs Away." In the American version, the forest animals make a figure out of tar, rather than birdlime, to outsmart Brer Rabbit.

Other slave tales were revisions of Bible stories, told from a black point of view. Some enslaved people retold the story of Cain and Abel, describing those sons of Adam and Eve as black men. When God placed a mark on Cain in the revised version, He gave Cain white skin.

Telling tales in the slave quarters at night was a way to teach young people morals and to tell them something about the natural world. Folk tales were survival lessons as well. Like the wily animal that outsmarts a stronger beast, clever slaves could sometimes get the best of their masters.

Slavery Is No More

By 1860, there were 3,954,000 enslaved workers living in the South. They accounted for nearly a third of the region's population. Some states had more slaves than free citizens. Enslaved African Americans made up 57 percent of the population in South Carolina and 55 percent in Mississippi. Conflict over the institution of slavery was about to tear the nation apart.

By March 1861, 11 southern states had left the Union to form a slaveholding nation of their own, the Confederate States of America. The first fighting of the Civil War occurred a month later, in the harbor of Charleston, South Carolina.

The North went to war primarily to repair the Union. But as news filtered down to the slaves, and they watched their masters go off to join regiments, they perceived that the days of slavery were numbered. Thousands of enslaved men fled their owners to serve in the Union forces. More than 200,000 African Americans—slaves and free men—fought for the United States in the Civil War. As Union troops occupied portions of the South, hundreds of thousands of enslaved women, children, and men abandoned the plantations for freedom.

The Confederate surrender on April 9, 1865, signaled the end of southern slavery. The Thirteenth Amendment to the Constitution, ratified on December 6, 1865, made slavery illegal throughout the United States. It seemed to millions of African Americans that a prophecy had come true. In towns and on farms, they raised their voices to sing:

> Shout the glad tidings o'er Egypt's dark sea,
> Jehovah has triumphed, his people are free!

NOTES

p. 35   "Negroes are too high . . ." Quoted in Ronald Segal, *The Black Diaspora* (New York: Farrar, Straus and Giroux, 1995), p. 57.

p. 36   "from using and carrying mischievous . . ." William A. Hotchkiss, comp., *A Codification of the Statute Law of Georgia, Including the English Statutes in Force* (Savannah, 1845), p. 813.

p. 36   "The slaves have Sunday . . ." Isaac Holmes, *An Account of the United States of America* (London: Caxton Press, 1823), p. 332.

p. 38   "Way down in the bottom . . ." Quoted in Lydia Parrish, *Slave Songs of the Georgia Sea Islands* (New York: Creative Age Press, 1942), p. 247.

p. 39   "A keen observer might . . ." Frederick Douglass, *The Life and Times of Frederick Douglass* (rev. ed. 1892; New York: Collier Books, 1962), p. 159.

p. 39 "I know moon-rise . . ." Quoted in Thomas Wentworth Higginson, *Army Life in a Black Regiment* (1869; New York: W.W. Norton and Company, 1984), p. 199.

p. 40 "Mass [Master] Jesus . . ." Quoted in Levine, in Harris, p. 102.

p. 41 "The way in which . . ." James L. Smith, *Autobiography of James L. Smith*. Norwich, Conn., 1881. Reprinted in Arna Bontemps, ed., *Five Black Lives* (Middleton, Conn.: Wesleyan University Press, 1971), p. 163.

p. 41 "The slave forgets all his . . ." Peter Randolph, *Sketches of Slave Life or, Illustrations of the Peculiar Institution* (Boston, 1855), pp. 30–31.

p. 42 "The belief in divination . . ." Quoted in Bill Broadway, "Digging Up Some Divining Inspiration," *Washington Post*, August 16, 1997, p. D7.

p. 43 "He early appeared . . ." W. E. B. Du Bois, "The Religion of the American Negro," *New World* (December 1900), p. 618.

p. 44 "there remain of the Mattoponies . . ." Quoted in J. H. Johnston, "Documentary Evidence of the Relations of Negroes and Indians," *Journal of Negro History* (January 1929), p. 33.

p. 44 "half Indian and half Negro." Quoted in Johnston, p. 41.

p. 45 "half Negro and half Indian . . . He plays . . ." Quoted in Johnston, p. 28.

p. 45 "Was born of an Indian woman . . ." Quoted in Johnston, p. 28.

p. 46 "You slaves will go to heaven . . ." Quoted in John B. Cade, "Out of the Mouths of Ex-Slaves," *Journal of Negro History* (July 1935), p. 329.

p. 47 "Shout the glad tidings . . ." Quoted in Albert J. Raboteau, *Fire in the Bones: Reflections on African-American Religious History* (Boston: Beacon Press, 1995), p. 34.

4

Toward a Better Place

The Diaspora Following Emancipation

Emancipation, like slavery, had a profound effect on the history of many American nations. With freedom, the former slaves gained mobility. Many moved from one region to another, seeking opportunity. The African diaspora grew more complex, and its influence more far-reaching.

The End of Slavery

Slavery was abolished first in Saint-Domingue, a French island colony (the western third of Hispaniola) with a large black majority. By 1790, Saint-Domingue's enslaved population exceeded 450,000. At the same time, three-fifths of the

> *Restored to our primitive dignity, we have asserted our rights; we swear never to yield to any power on earth. The frightful veil of prejudice is torn to pieces. Be it so forever! Woe be to them who would dare to put together its bloody tatters!*
>
>
>
> —Jean-Jacques Dessalines proclaiming independence of Saint-Domingue (November 28, 1803)

colony's 54,000 free citizens were of African descent. Taking advantage of conflicts within the planter class, the slaves revolted in 1791. Strong leaders soon emerged to guide the rebellion, urging slaves and free blacks to burn plantations and take over property. The best known was François Dominique Toussaint Louverture (c. 1743–1803), who led the defense of the revolution against British and Spanish invaders and named himself governor for life in 1801.

A year later, Napoléon Bonaparte dispatched French forces to Saint-Domingue with orders to remove Toussaint Louverture from power and take back the colony. The soldiers captured Toussaint Louverture by trickery and shipped him to France in chains. His followers kept fighting, though, and soon defeated the French. On November 29, 1803, Toussaint Louverture's lieutenant, Jean-Jacques Dessalines, declared the independence of Saint-Domingue. Dessalines crowned himself emperor of the Western Hemisphere's second independent republic, which was to be called Haiti.

In 1833, Britain's Parliament passed a bill abolishing slavery in most British colonies, effective August 1, 1834. Under the new law, slave owners were reimbursed for the property they were losing. Enslaved workers were required to spend four years as apprentices to their old masters before gaining their freedom. There were many reports of harsh treatment, including beatings, during the apprenticeship period.

Slaves in the Spanish and Portuguese colonies were straining for freedom in the 19th century while the colonies themselves struggled for political independence. In Mexico,

Central America, Colombia, and elsewhere, emancipation accompanied national independence or came soon afterward. Brazil was the last New World nation to end slavery, doing so in 1888.

Harsh New Realities

Life changed little for most enslaved workers after they gained their freedom. Throughout the hemisphere, blacks continued doing the work they had done as slaves, which was likely to be plantation farming.

Most former slaves in the United States continued to live in the South and raised cotton, sugar, tobacco, and grains. Only one in four owned any amount of land. The rest were tenant farmers, leasing their fields from white landowners.

Many African Americans farmed cotton after emancipation, much as they had under slavery. (The Library of Congress)

If they paid their landlords with produce, they were known as sharecroppers. Tenant farmers barely scraped by. They possessed some clothing, a few household items, and not much more. They were often in debt.

Following the Civil War, the government sought to restore normal relations with the states that had seceded and so undertook a program known as Reconstruction. Some prominent African Americans joined the effort with the goal of assisting the newly freed slaves. For example, Dr. Martin Delany, the U.S. Army's first black major, worked with the Freedmen's Bureau. This government agency provided food, medical care, and schooling to African Americans and helped them adjust to life after slavery. Francis L. Cardozo, a Congregational minister, founded teacher-training programs for blacks in the South.

But the white planter class quickly reasserted control. As soon as new state governments were formed, they passed "black codes," laws aimed at preventing African Americans from making social or economic progress. The black codes, for example, indicated where African Americans could live or buy land and required black men to take low-paying jobs offered by whites—or risk arrest for vagrancy. Fear of further such laws prompted many northerners to support the Fifteenth Amendment to the Constitution, which established that no state could deny any man the right to vote "on account of race, color, or previous condition of servitude." (The Constitution did not protect a woman's right to vote until 1920.)

With the vote, and with federal troops still stationed in the South, African Americans exercised their voice in politics and took part in public life. They were elected to state legislatures and hired as police officers. Cities with large black populations, such as Beaufort, South Carolina, chose black mayors. Two black men were elected to the U.S. Senate, and 20 served in the House of Representatives. African Americans used the political system to build schools and railroad lines and to aid the poor. It was during this period that such outstanding black colleges as Fisk Free School (now Fisk University) in Nashville, Tennessee, and Howard University in Washington, D.C., were founded.

But in 1877, the last army units withdrew from the South, and African Americans saw their gains erode. White conservatives took control of state and local governments and passed the infamous Jim Crow legislation, making segregation the law of the land in the South. Poll taxes and unfair literacy tests suddenly made it nearly impossible for poor blacks to vote.

Certain southerners thought the laws failed to go far enough in suppressing the black population. These white supremacists banded together in secret organizations such as the Knights of the White Camelia and the Ku Klux Klan. They used threats and terrorism to keep African Americans from exercising their rights or striving to get ahead.

Kansas Fever

From its first years as a nation, the United States had been expanding westward. Settlers had been clearing fields and building towns west of the Appalachian Mountains, along the Mississippi River, and beyond. Thousands of African Americans joined the push west following the Civil War. From Kentucky and Tennessee, from Mississippi and Louisiana, black pioneers journeyed toward a better life.

Many headed for Kansas, lured by the preaching of leaders such as Benjamin "Pap" Singleton. The way things stood in the South, Singleton told his people, "whites had the land and the sense and the blacks had nothing but their freedom." Singleton, a former slave, taught that God had a plan in mind for Kansas. It was to be a place where black society existed apart from whites but interacted with them peacefully. Singleton's followers founded two communities in Kansas. The larger one, Nicodemus, was settled by black pioneers from Kentucky. There were 700 African Americans in Nicodemus in 1880, and 15,000 in the state of Kansas. African Americans also put down roots in Nevada, Utah, and other western states and territories. Some lived in remote locations, separated from other members of their race by many miles.

The history of the American West is enlivened by the exploits of many colorful, plucky characters. One such person was Clara Brown, an enslaved woman who purchased her freedom in 1859. Eager for adventure, Brown went west as a cook with a party of gold prospectors. She started a laundry business in Colorado, where she worked hard and set aside her profits. She saved enough money to bring 34 of her relatives to Denver after the Civil War. In the years that followed, she outfitted many more African Americans for the trip west.

I work in Swifts packing Co. in the sausage department. My daughter and I work for the same company—We get $1.50 a day and we pack so many sausages we dont have much time to play but it is a matter of a dollar with me and I feel that God made the path and I am walking therein.

—A Chicago worker's letter to a sister in the South (1917)

Moving North

In 1900, 6 million African Americans—nine-tenths of the black population—lived in the South. But industrial jobs and new rail routes were luring people north. Black communities of 50,000 or more already existed in Boston, New York, Philadelphia, and other northern cities. Most residents earned their wages as laborers or servants, but a small number were business owners, doctors, lawyers, and teachers.

Men, many newly arrived from the South, crowd the Chicago Employment Office in 1920. (Chicago Urban League Records, Special Collections, The University Library, University of Illinois at Chicago)

In 1916, many more African Americans began to go north. An infestation of boll weevils was destroying much of the southern cotton crop and forcing farmers off the land. At the same time, World War I dried up the flow of immigrants from Europe, and northern factories lost their chief source of labor. African Americans saw an opportunity for advancement. Life in the North promised steady work, improved schools, and greater rights. "Anywhere north will do us and I suppose the worst place there is better than the best place here," reasoned a black worker in New Orleans.

Between 1916 and 1918, when the First World War ended, more than 400,000 southern blacks had packed up and headed north. One million more would move north in the decade after the war. The urge to leave was so strong that some small towns were virtually emptied of people. Church

Building a Canal

At the beginning of the 20th century, the United States was about to undertake a mammoth project: construction of the Panama Canal. The completed canal would connect the Atlantic and Pacific Oceans. It would be more than 40 miles long and 41 feet deep at its shallowest point. Its locks would be large enough to handle oceangoing vessels.

The job required an enormous number of workers, and President Theodore Roosevelt was ready to hire any worker who could "make the dirt fly." Panama's population of 400,000 was too small to provide enough hands, so people came from other places to meet the demand. White and black Americans headed south to join the workforce. Laborers came from the Basque Provinces of Spain. But the largest number of workers were people of African descent from the West Indies. Between 150,000 and 200,000 West Indians migrated to Panama between 1904 and the opening of the canal 10 years later.

Why did so many West Indians come? In places

A ship carrying West Indian laborers docks in Cristobal, Panama (The National Archives)

pews went unoccupied. "A Negro minister may have all his deacons with him at the mid week meeting but by Sunday every church officer is likely to be in the North," reported a government researcher.

such as Barbados, Martinique, and Curaçao, unemployment was high and people were destitute. Many knew they must leave the islands or face starvation. When U.S. recruiters offered them 500 days' work in Panama at 10¢ an hour, men eagerly signed up. The most they could earn on a sugar plantation was 20¢ a day—if they found a job. The governor of Jamaica, meanwhile, refused to allow recruiters on that island. Nevertheless, word got around, and 20,000 Jamaicans paid their own way to Panama.

Most of the Jamaicans who came were skilled artisans, but their abilities failed to impress the white American supervisors. Skin color mattered most, and black workers were assigned to the dirtiest, most dangerous work. They dug 1.75 million cubic yards of earth and loaded it into flatbed railroad cars. They cut down giant trees and demolished the trunks with dynamite. The West Indian laborers carted heavy loads of lumber and cement. "Life was some sort of semislavery," one worker said.

Panama was hot, muddy, and buggy. Landslides were a constant danger, and so were malaria and yellow fever, diseases carried by mosquitoes. Accidents took many lives. During the first 10 months of 1906, the death rate among West Indians in Panama was 59 per every 1,000 workers. The death rate among whites was only 17 per every 1,000 workers.

Much of the black workforce lived in the slums of Colón at the northern entrance to the canal. People slept in crowded firetraps or in shacks built on stilts. Beneath the shacks was "a morass," the *New York Tribune* reported in 1904, "a vast expanse of black water covered with green scum."

Women came to Panama from the islands, too. Although they did not have a hand in building the canal, their work made the laborers' lives easier to bear. The women cooked meals, washed clothes, and nursed the sick. Men and women married and had families.

A large number of workers remained in Panama after the canal was completed, and a West Indian community took hold. Its members are proud of their forebears, whose hard work and sacrifices made possible one of the greatest engineering feats of all time.

This redistribution of people—one of the largest in the nation's history—is known as the Great Migration. It was "The Flight Out of Egypt," announced the black press, recalling the slaves' identification with the children of Israel.

The newcomers stepped off trains in cities throughout the North, but especially in Chicago, Illinois, known for its many factories and huge meatpacking industry. Chicago had a black population of 44,000 in 1910. That number had grown to 109,000 10 years later.

The dream of the good life never quite came true for most black migrants. Companies hired them to fill low-level jobs that offered little chance of getting ahead. Unwelcome in many white neighborhoods, they paid high rents for small, rundown apartments that often lacked stoves and toilets. Poverty and overcrowding led to high rates of tuberculosis, pneumonia, and other diseases. The death rate for urban blacks was higher than for whites, and the infant mortality rate was alarming. One city, Philadelphia, recorded 150 deaths among every 1,000 black infants born in the first years of the Great Migration. The rate for white babies in the same period was 92.8 deaths per 1,000 births.

In the summer of 1919, race riots occurred in 26 U.S. cities. White soldiers returning from the war feared competition from African Americans for jobs and clashed with a black population unhappy with life in the North. White mobs murdered several black citizens in Washington, D.C., and tried to burn down a black neighborhood. In Chicago, an African-American swimmer drowned after whites threw rocks at him from the shore of Lake Michigan; the incident sparked a week of fighting between black and white gangs in Chicago, leaving 38 dead and 537 injured. White America was quick to forget that 400,000 African Americans had also served in the armed forces in World War I.

Migration in Central and South America

The ending of slavery led to population shifts throughout the Americas as former slaves and their descendants hoped to gain opportunities and improve their living conditions.

In a movement similar to the Great Migration in the United States, millions of people of African descent abandoned Brazilian farming regions and traveled to the nation's cities. There, they discovered that white business owners preferred to hire the European immigrants who were arriving daily. Black Brazilians had no choice but to take menial jobs for meager pay.

Caribbean laborers moved from island to island in search of work. Between 1913 and 1928, Cuban sugar producers recruited 400,000 people from Jamaica and Haiti. The United Fruit Company of the Dominican Republic and Central America hired many West Indian immigrants, as did the United States Sugar Company of Florida. Before the passage of strict U.S. immigration laws in the 1920s, 130,000 people moved from Caribbean nations to the United States. Many settled in New York City.

A Second Wave

When the United States entered World War II in December 1941, African Americans were eager to join the war effort. Thousands of black men and women enlisted in the army and the navy, where they served in segregated units. (During the course of the war, 1 million African Americans joined the armed forces.) Many others sought jobs in defense industries, knowing manufacturers needed workers to build ships, planes, and tanks. More than 50,000 students at traditionally black colleges signed up for training that would prepare them for defense work.

But the jobs all went to whites. Companies such as Boeing Aircraft refused to put African Americans on their payrolls, and labor unions restricted their membership to whites.

"I think we ought to get 10,000 Negroes and march down Pennsylvania Avenue asking for jobs in defense plants and integration of the armed forces," said black labor leader A. Philip Randolph. As African Americans voiced strong support for his idea, Randolph enlarged his plans and called for 100,000 people to march past the White House. Government leaders, alarmed at the thought of so many African Americans descending upon segregated Washington, D.C., hurried to appease black America. President Franklin Roosevelt

Inglewood, California, 1942: North American Aviation employees construct the wing of a B-25 bomber. (The Library of Congress)

issued an executive order to "encourage full participation in the national defense programme by all citizens . . . regardless of race." He established the Fair Employment Practices Committee to make sure that companies complied with the order. The president had stopped short of ending segregation in the military, but Randolph was satisfied enough to call off the march. The United States would not begin integrating its fighting forces until 1948.

With the door to employment open, many African Americans took defense-industry jobs along the coasts of the Atlantic Ocean and the Gulf of Mexico. An estimated 1.6 million African Americans left the South for other parts of the country. Because millions of men were called up by the armed forces, many women—both African American and white—held jobs in heavy industry for the first time. "Hitler was the one that got us out of the white folks' kitchen," one black woman joked.

Factories on the West Coast were also operating at full capacity. African Americans moved to California, Oregon, and Washington to build ships and aircraft for the war effort in the Pacific. Approximately 340,000 African Americans went to California during World War II. Most settled in Los Angeles, in established black neighborhoods. In 1943, 10,000 African Americans arrived in Los Angeles every month. San Francisco's black population grew 600 percent during the war, and Seattle's nearly tripled.

Wherever they moved, however, equal treatment still eluded African-American workers. In Bremerton, Washington, for example, federal housing officials assigned black families to segregated housing projects. The Boilermakers' Union collected dues from black members throughout the war but barred them from voting in union elections. Race riots broke out in New York City, Detroit, Chicago, and East St. Louis, Illinois.

Despite the violence and discrimination, African Americans made measurable gains. Not a single black laborer had worked in the defense industries in 1941. By the time the war ended, in 1945, African Americans accounted for a significant part of the defense-industry workforce. More than 7 percent of the workers at one large company, Lockheed Aircraft, were black.

Migration from the South continued after the war, with nearly 3 million African Americans moving north during the 1950s and 1960s. By 1970, 50 years after the onset of the Great Migration, the majority of African Americans lived outside the South.

West Indians on the Move

West Indians kept moving as well, because large growers were taking over independent plantations in the Caribbean. As the growers consolidated operations in the 1940s, they needed fewer workers. In Trinidad and Barbados, as in neighboring island nations, more than half of the islands' workers held jobs in agriculture before World War II. By the late 1940s, agriculture employed just 22.8 percent of workers in Trinidad and 16.7 percent in Barbados.

Many West Indians immigrated to the United States and, beginning in the 1960s, to Canada. Others settled in Great Britain. Britain's Nationality Act of 1948 granted citizenship to the people of British colonies. As British citizens, these people were free to enter Britain without restrictions and to stay as long as they wished. Over the next 10 years, Britain witnessed the arrival of 125,000 West Indians and a smaller number of Africans.

And so the African diaspora evolves. West Indians are still settling in Britain and North America. Descendants of African slaves are among the many Cubans who have left their country under Fidel Castro's regime for New York City or Miami, Florida. As the people of the diaspora put down roots and make new lives, they enrich the cultures of their chosen homes.

NOTES

p. 50 "Restored to our primitive . . ." Quoted in John Hope Franklin, *From Slavery to Freedom: A History of Negro Americans,* 3d. ed. (New York: Alfred A. Knopf, 1967), p. 346.

p. 53 "whites had the land . . ." Quoted in Berry and Blassingame, p. 403.

p. 54 "I work in Swifts . . ." Quoted in Emmett J. Scott, comp., "Additional Letters of Negro Migrants of 1916–1918," *Journal of Negro History* (October 1919), p. 457.

p. 55 "Anywhere north will do . . ." Quoted in Scott, p. 442.

p. 56 "make the dirt fly." Quoted in Michael L. Conniff, *Black Labor on a White Canal: Panama, 1904–1981* (Pittsburgh: University of Pittsburgh Press, 1985), p. 25.

p. 56 "A Negro minister may have . . ." George Haynes, *Negro Migration in 1916–1917* (Washington, D.C.: U.S. Department of Labor, Division of Negro Economics, U.S. Government Printing Office, 1919), p. 12.

p. 57 "Life was some sort of semislavery." Quoted in Conniff, p. 38.

p. 57 "a morass . . ." Quoted in David McCullough, *The Path Between the Seas: The Creation of the Panama Canal, 1870–1914* (New York: Simon and Schuster, 1977), p. 406.

pp. 59–60 "I think we ought to . . ." Quoted in Paula F. Pfeffer, *A. Philip Randolph, Pioneer of the Civil Rights Movement* (Baton Rouge, La.: Louisiana State University Press, 1990), p. 47.

p. 61 "encourage full participation . . ." Quoted in Segal, p. 251.

p. 61 "Hitler was the one . . ." Quoted in Richard White, *"It's Your Misfortune and None of My Own": A New History of the American West* (Norman, Okla.: University of Oklahoma Press, 1991), p. 506.

5

Riffs, Runs, and Breaks
The Spoken and Written Word

When present-day Jamaicans refer to *nyam-nyam* (food) or describe a recent *kas-kas* (quarrel), they are using words that survive unchanged from the Twi language of West Africa. English may be the official language of Jamaica, but many residents use the regional creole, which combines English and African elements.

Creoles remain the first languages of people throughout the African diaspora. They are remnants of African culture in the New World, heirlooms from the time when slaves first arrived in the Americas. Most Haitians understand Patois, the regional French creole. Another French creole, Gombo, is still spoken in parts of Louisiana. Two creoles live on in Surinam: One, derived from English, is the language of the Bush Negroes, descendants of a maroon population; the other is Dutch-based, a survival from the 17th century, when the Netherlands controlled the island.

Creoles tend to have more in common with one another than with the languages from which they were derived. That is why Louisiana's Gombo can be understood by Haitians but not by speakers of Standard French. The same holds true for English-based creoles and users of Standard English.

How Creoles Are Alike

A word that begins with a cluster of consonants in a European language is likely to lose one of those consonants in a creole. Thus, the English word *split* became *plit* in Jamaican creole. Syntax, or the order of words in sentences, often follows an African pattern. For example, some creole speakers place definite articles (e.g., *the,* in English, or *le* or *la,* in French) and demonstrative articles (e.g., *this* or *that* in English, or *este* or *esse,* in Portuguese) after a noun instead of before it. Such a pattern is consistent with the Ewe and Wolof languages.

Linguists have debated about Africa's influence on language in the United States. Clearly Africanisms persist in Gombo and in Gullah, the creole spoken in the Sea Islands, off the coasts of South Carolina, Georgia, and Florida, where enslaved Africans had little contact with whites or free blacks. Researchers have counted more than 4,000 words

It is absurd to assume, as has been the tendency, among a great many Western anthropologists and sociologists, that all traces of Africa were erased from the Negro's mind because he learned English. The very nature of the English the Negro spoke and still speaks drops the lie on that idea.

◆

—LeRoi Jones (Imamu Amiri Baraka), *Blues People* (1963)

from 21 African languages in the speech of the Gullah, as the people of the Sea Islands have come to be called, too. As late as 1940, many Gullah answered to English names when dealing with whites but used African names with one another.

The debate centers on African retentions in everyday American English speech. Some linguists insist that the African influence was very slight. Decreolization was so thorough in the United States, they say, that nearly all traces of African and creole speech have disappeared. The number of English words with African origins is small—fewer than 150, according to one source. They include *okra, zombie,* and the verb *tote,* "to carry." The word *banana* survives unchanged from the Wolof language of West Africa. The name of Bambi, the beloved fawn of story and film, comes from a Bantu word, *mubambi,* used to describe an antelope fawn concealing itself. And *hepcat,* which sounds as if it should be a slang word invented in the United States, is actually derived from the Wolof word *hipicat,* meaning a man in the know, or a man with his eyes open.

Other linguists assert that the speech of many African Americans is different enough from Standard English to qualify as a separate language. They call this language Black English, or Ebonics.

Ebonics employs English vocabulary, but it resembles creole languages in some ways. The question in Standard English "What does he do?" becomes *What he do?* in Ebonics. The same question takes a similar form— *Wa im do?*—in Jamaican creole. Ebonics also reflects its speakers' African roots. Use of the word done to indicate past tense, as in "I done gone," occurring in Ebonics and in the speech of some southern whites, is similar to the way past action is expressed in several African languages.

The Literature of African Americans

The enslaved people and their descendants have left their mark on written language as well. In their prose and poetry, African-American writers describe many aspects of the diaspora experience.

Although laws made it a crime to teach enslaved Africans to read and write, a number of whites instructed their slaves in those skills. Other enslaved people picked up reading and writing on their own. Those who showed literary talent and managed to escape slavery found an audience that was curious to read about their experiences. Many of the earliest published works by African Americans are narratives of slave life. The autobiographies of Olaudah Equiano (c. 1745–97) and Frederick Douglass (1817–95) belong to this tradition.

Douglass's 1845 book *Narrative of the Life of Frederick Douglass, an American Slave* describes a childhood spent in slavery on a Talbot County, Maryland, plantation and in a Baltimore home. In its pages, Douglass recalled his secret effort to learn to read and write. He told of his cruel treatment at the hands of a slave breaker, a man hired to crush the spirit of any slave with a rebellious nature.

Douglass eventually escaped to freedom in Massachusetts, but most enslaved workers were less fortunate. He wrote movingly about his grandmother, who had served her owner "faithfully from youth to old age." After the master and his wife died, Douglass's grandmother saw her family members separated and sold "like so many sheep," Douglass wrote. The old woman could no longer work, so she was banished to a hut in the woods to await her death. "If my poor old grandmother now lives, she lives to suffer in utter loneliness," Douglass stated. "She lives to remember and mourn over the loss of children, the loss of grandchildren, and the loss of great-grandchildren."

Booker T. Washington's autobiography, *Up From Slavery* (1901), continued the narrative tradition. Washington (1856–1915) described his childhood in slavery, his efforts to get an education, and his work as a spokesman for black America. As founder of the Tuskegee Institute, a vocational school for African Americans, Washington believed that blacks could advance only gradually in American society. He advocated trades and service occupations for African Americans, rather than academic pursuits. He urged the men and women of his race to remain in rural settings.

Rebirth in Harlem

By 1916, Booker T. Washington was dead. With jobs and a better life awaiting them in northern cities, many people felt that his thinking was behind the times. Among the thousands who moved north during the Great Migration were writers, artists, and musicians. They came together in urban communities, especially in New York City's Harlem. The inspiration that was generated when these creative people shared ideas gave rise to an artistic and literary movement known as the Harlem Renaissance.

Between the two world wars, writers of the Harlem Renaissance presented many aspects of African-American thought and experience in their work. "The pulse of the Negro world has begun to beat in Harlem," proclaimed the scholar Alain Locke.

Claude McKay (1890–1948), a poet who arrived in Harlem in 1912, expressed the weary anger felt by black persons in a racist society. "Oh I must search for wisdom every hour, / Deep in my wrathful bosom sore and raw," he wrote, "And find in it the superhuman power / To hold me to the letter of the law." The Jamaican-born McKay described the homesickness of West Indian immigrants in

Claude McKay   (The Library of Congress)

Nicolás Guillén: Poet of African Cuba

When Nicolás Guillén began to write poems in the 1920s, he used traditional forms, such as the sonnet, that white Spanish poets had long employed. Like many Cubans with African blood, Guillén considered himself mulatto, a term that acknowledged his mixed African and European heritage. Yet he ignored the African side of himself, striving to be as Spanish as Cuba's white majority. White Cubans saw his blackness, however, and looked down on him for it.

In 1930, Langston Hughes visited Cuba. Meeting the American poet was a revelation for Guillén. Here was a man who looked like a Cuban mulatto but proudly called himself black. "This great Black poet," Guillén noted, was "one of the souls most interested in the black race." He read Hughes's poetry avidly, observing how the American writer found subject matter and rhythms in his people and their music.

Guillén was determined to do for black Cubans what Hughes and other writers had done for African Americans. Cuban writing needed an "African shot-in-the-arm," he said, a reminder of the African presence within the nation. He stopped using traditional Spanish forms. He looked for rhythms in a kind of Afro-Cuban music known as *son* (literally

northern U.S. cities. He wrote of seeing island produce—"Bananas ripe and green, and ginger-root"—in a Harlem store window. McKay concluded, "A wave of longing through my body swept, . . . I turned aside and bowed my head and wept."

Countee Cullen (1903–46) was born in Louisville, Kentucky, but raised in Harlem. He wrote thoughtful poems that explored his African roots and his mission as a poet. Like McKay, Cullen used traditional meters, rhyme schemes, and vocabulary in his work.

Langston Hughes, in contrast, filled his poetry with the rhythms of African-American music and the language of workaday life. He compared his writing to "the riffs, runs,

"sound" in Spanish), and he called on Cubans of African descent to take pride in their race, to "Shine in [their] blackness . . ."

Guillén's poetry also carries a political message. He was born in 1902, the year in which the Republic of Cuba was established. The new nation's constitution gave unusual political and economic power to the United States, which had financial interests in Cuba. Growing up, Guillén watched U.S. companies exploit Cuban workers, and he came to embrace communism.

The poems of Guillén have been translated into more than 30 languages. Poets and novelists throughout the African diaspora acknowledge their debt to him. Because of his influence, Latin American literature will never be strictly white or European again.

Guillén left Cuba in 1953, living first in Chile and then in Paris. He returned to his homeland in 1959, after Fidel Castro seized power on the island. Guillén then abandoned his call for black pride because it was no longer necessary: All Cubans would have full equality under Castro, he preached. He dreamed of a new way of life in Latin America, of a *mulatez* society, one in which people of African, European, and Indian descent blended biologically and culturally. He envisioned "A black face and a white face . . . crowned by the same fraternal laurel."

Nicolás Guillén died in 1989. His was a long and noteworthy career.

breaks, and disc-tortions of the music of a community in transition."

The best-known poet of the Harlem Renaissance, Hughes was born in Missouri in 1902. He attended Lincoln University in Pennsylvania and worked as a busboy, a seaman, a teacher, and a journalist before gaining prominence as a writer.

Hughes's poetry conveys his outrage at the unfair treatment of blacks in American society. At the same time, it portrays ordinary African-American characters and presents scenes from their lives. In "Mother to Son," for example, a woman counsels her child to expect a hard life: "Well, son, I'll tell you: / Life for me ain't been no crystal stair."

Hughes wrote often about the "dream deferred," the hope or ambition postponed indefinitely because of social forces such as racism. In the poem "Harlem [2]," he wonders whether such a dream might "dry up / like a raisin in the

Zora Neale Hurston (The Library of Congress)

sun," or sag "like a heavy load." In a verse alluding to the racial violence of America's cities, he asks, *"Or does it explode?"*

Hughes, who died in 1967, published more than 40 books, beginning with the poetry collection *Weary Blues* (1926). He wrote verse, short stories, film scripts, essays, a novel, and an autobiography. He coauthored the play *Mule Bone* with Zora Neale Hurston (1891–1960).

Hurston, a Florida native, arrived penniless in New York City in 1925. An ambitious person, she had spent six years working her way through Howard University in Washington, D.C. She quickly found a job in New York, met a group of writer friends, and secured a scholarship to Columbia University. There, she entered a new scientific field, anthropology. Anthropologists study the physical features and cultures of peoples throughout the world.

Hurston's studies took her to Florida, New Orleans, Jamaica, and Haiti. On those trips she collected folk tales from people of the African diaspora. What she heard inspired her, and she incorporated folklore into her novels, stories, and plays. Her books include the novel *Their Eyes Were Watching God* (1937) and an autobiography, *Dust Tracks on a Road* (1942).

Writing After World War II

By the time the United States entered World War II, the Harlem Renaissance had lost momentum. But African-American writers never stopped drawing on their experiences and cultural heritage to create outstanding literature.

Mississippi-born Richard Wright (1908–60) reached a large interracial audience with his best-selling novel *Native Son*. Published in 1940, *Native Son* probed the mind of a young black man through the story of Bigger Thomas, a well-known character in American literature.

Growing up in a Chicago ghetto under the constant shadow of racism turns Bigger into a person motivated by fear and anger. Bigger gets a break when a wealthy white family hires him as a chauffeur. While on the job one night, he carries the family's drunken daughter to her room. He panics at the thought of being discovered by her bed, sure that no one will believe his reason for being there. Muffling the girl's moans, he accidentally kills her. Bigger kills again when he fears that his girlfriend will reveal his hiding place. Eventually, he is arrested, tried, and sentenced to death. Wright called *Native Son* "an accusation against the society of the United States and a defense of the Negro people, who still live in conditions very similar to slavery."

In 1945, Wright published the autobiographical novel *Black Boy*, about a young African American in the South and

Richard Wright stands outside a Paris bookstore, 1948. (The University of Mississippi)

his unrelenting struggle to escape his environment. Two years later, Wright decided that he, too, needed to escape. He moved with his family to Paris, France, where he was not judged by his race. Wright continued to produce books, but they never achieved the success of his earlier work.

The novelist James Baldwin (1924–87) also found acceptance in Paris, where he took up residence in 1948. He moved back to the United States 10 years later and quickly involved himself in the growing civil rights movement. Baldwin wrote several highly regarded novels, beginning with *Go Tell It on the Mountain* (1953). This book explores a Harlem youth's emotional life, examining his religious conversion and his troubled relationship with his stepfather. Baldwin based much of the story on his own early years.

Baldwin was an eloquent essayist as well. He published several essay collections, including *Notes of a Native Son* (1955) and *The Fire Next Time* (1963), an immediate bestseller. Baldwin's essays cover a broad range of topics. Some offer insightful commentary on race relations; others reminisce about life in Harlem or in Paris, or discuss the books of his fellow writers, including Richard Wright.

Throughout his work, Baldwin elaborates on two ideas put forth in *Notes of a Native Son.* "The first idea was acceptance," he wrote, "of life as it is, and men as they are: in the light of this idea, it goes without saying that injustice is commonplace." The second idea was "that one must never . . . accept these injustices as commonplace but must fight them with all one's strength."

Ralph Ellison (1914–94) brought racial issues to the attention of mainstream America with his single major work of fiction, *Invisible Man* (1952). Ellison's main character remains nameless, a being ignored by white society. "When they approach me they see only my surroundings, themselves, or figments of their imagination—indeed, everything and anything except me," Ellison's protagonist says, giving voice to the author's observation that whites ignore the individuality of their black fellow Americans.

Contemporary Women Writers

In recent decades, a number of African-American women writers have gained prominence by presenting black life from a female—and often feminist—point of view.

Alice Walker (born 1944) explores family relationships in her poetry and fiction. Personal growth is another important theme for her. Walker's best-known novel, *The Color Purple* (1982), describes the different journeys of two African-American sisters from lives of hardship in the rural South toward understanding and the full use of their talents.

Ntozake Shange (born 1948) is known best for her theater piece *For Colored Girls Who Have Considered Suicide / When the Rainbow Is Enuf* (1974). Shange calls this work a "choreopoem." It is a pastiche of music, dance, prose, and poetry that explores what it means to be a black woman in American society. Paule Marshall (born 1929) looks at the lives of West Indian immigrants in *Brown Girl, Brownstones* (1959) and other books, while Jamaica Kincaid (born 1949) returns to her native Antigua in novels such as *Annie John* (1985).

In 1993, America's foremost black woman writer, Toni Morrison, was awarded the Nobel Prize for Literature. The prize honored not one book but an entire body of work. In her fiction Morrison (born 1931) often employs myths and folklore from the

*T*ell us what it is to be a woman so that we may know what it is to be a man. What moves at the margin. What it is to have no home on this place. To be set adrift from the one you knew. What it is to live at the edge of towns that cannot bear your company.

◆

—Toni Morrison, in her Nobel Prize acceptance speech, 1993

African-American tradition, including the appearance of supernatural beings. *Tar Baby* (1981) uses the well-known story of Brer Rabbit as a metaphor for the unworkable relationship between a couple on a small West Indian island. The ghost that haunts *Beloved* (1987) is that of a murdered child.

Morrison has said that her themes—love, death, guilt, acceptance, survival—have always occupied writers' minds and will continue to do so. They appear in the narratives of enslaved people, in the poems of the Harlem Renaissance, and in the novels of authors writing today. As Morrison reminds us, "The subjects that are important in the world are the same ones that have always been important."

NOTES

p. 65 "It is absurd . . ." LeRoi Jones, *Blues People* (New York: William Morrow and Company, 1963), p. 9.

p. 67 "faithfully from youth to old age."; "like so many sheep."; and "If my poor old grandmother . . ." Frederick Douglass, *Narrative of the Life of Frederick Douglass, an American Slave* (1845; New York: Anchor Books, 1989), pp. 49–50.

p. 68 "The pulse of the Negro . . ." Alain Locke, "Enter the New Negro," *Survey Graphic* (March 1925), p. 633.

p. 68 "Oh I must search . . ." Claude McKay, "The White House," *Selected Poems of Claude McKay* (San Diego: Harcourt Brace Jovanovich, 1953), p. 78.

p. 70 "This great black poet . . ." Quoted in Richard L. Jackson, *Black Writers in Latin America* (Albuquerque: University of New Mexico Press, 1979), p. 88.

p. 70 "African shot-in-the-arm." Quoted in Jackson, p. 83.

p. 70 "Bananas ripe and green . . ." McKay, "The Tropics in New York," *Selected Poems of Claude McKay*, p. 31.

pp. 70–71 "the riffs, runs, breaks . . ." Langston Hughes, *The Langston Hughes Reader* (New York: Braziller, 1958), p. 89.

p. 71 "Shine in [their] blackness . . ." Nicolás Guillén, "Little Ode," *Cuba Libre: Poems by Nicolás Guillén,* Langston Hughes and Ben Frederick Carruthers, trans. (Los Angeles: The Ward Ritchie Press, 1948), p. 70.

p. 71 "A black face . . ." Guillén, "Thus Sings a Mockingbird in el Turquino," *Man-making Words: Selected Poems of Nicolás Guillén,* Robert Marquez and David Arthur Murray, trans. (University of Massachusetts Press, 1972), p. 185.

p. 71 "Well, son, I'll tell you . . ." Hughes, "Mother to Son," *Collected Poems of Langston Hughes* (New York: Vintage Books, 1994), p. 30.

p. 72–73 "dry up / like a raisin . . ." Hughes, "Harlem [2]," *Collected Poems of Langston Hughes,* p. 426.

p. 74 "an accusation against the society . . ." Quoted in Keneth Kinnamon and Michael Fabre, eds., *Conversations with Richard Wright* (Jackson: University Press of Mississippi, 1993), p. 32.

p. 75 "The first idea was acceptance . . ." James Baldwin, *Notes of a Native Son* (New York: The Dial Press, 1963), p. 102.

p. 75 "When they approach me . . ." Ralph Ellison, *Invisible Man* (New York: Vintage Books, 1980), p. 3.

p. 76 "Tell us what it is . . ." Toni Morrison, "Nobel Lecture 1993," *World Literature Today* (Winter 1994), p. 8.

p. 77 "The subjects that are important . . ." Quoted in Claudia Tate, ed., *Black Women Writers at Work* (New York: Continuum, 1989), p. 121.

6

The African Pulse

Music, Dance, and Visual Art of African America

One day in 1903, a black bandleader named W. C. Handy was dozing in the Tutwiler, Mississippi, train station when a strange song disturbed his rest. Handy opened his eyes to see that "a lean, loose-jointed Negro had commenced plunking a guitar next to me while I slept. His clothes were rags; his feet peeped out of his shoes. His face had on it some of the sadness of the ages."

The man sang a simple song about the town of Moorhead, where he was headed. He made up the tune as he went along. It was "the weirdest music I ever heard," Handy recalled. The odd song lingered in Handy's mind. It was like the work songs of field hands that he had listened to as a boy in

Florence, Alabama. On that day in 1903, W. C. Handy was introduced to the blues.

This lean, lanky guitar player was a drifter, like most early blues singers. Hitching rides, he moved from one place to another. He sang at parties and on street corners, always on the black side of town. His songs were full of "swoops" and "slurs"—the flat notes and sorrowful tones of African-American spirituals. But he sang about life's worries, and not about religion. Hard work, poverty, and love gone wrong were the subjects of the blues.

The blues began as folk music. No one wrote out the notes of blues songs. Musicians made tunes up, taught them to one another, and stored a great many songs in their heads. The blues gained a wider audience when W. C. Handy began to compose his own songs and to write them down. In 1912, Handy published an original composition, "Memphis Blues." Blacks and whites alike could not get enough of this stirring music. It was "the stuff the people wanted," Handy said. "It hit the spot." In 1914, Handy published "St. Louis Blues," a huge hit that made the blues a worldwide phenomenon.

> Southern Negroes sang about everything. Trains, steamboats, steam whistles, sledge hammers, fast women, mean bosses, stubborn mules—all become subjects for their songs. They accompany themselves on anything from which they can extract a musical sound or rhythmical effect, anything from a harmonica to a washboard. In this way, and from these materials, they set the mood for what we now call the blues.
>
> ◆
>
> —W. C. Handy, *Father of the Blues* (1941)

Piano Rags

African Americans were inventing another kind of music in the early years of the blues. This music was anything but sad. It was fast, complicated, and bouncy. It was played on a piano, and it was known as ragtime.

Enslaved people played a variety of instruments, but very few African Americans learned to play the piano until after the Civil War. Black musicians quickly discovered that they could do things on a keyboard that they could not begin to do on other instruments. Each of their hands could range separately over the keys, producing creative chords and melodies.

Nineteenth-century black pianists had a sophisticated knowledge of rhythm that came from their African heritage. It was only logical that they coaxed complex rhythms from the piano. In ragtime, the pianist's right hand hopped around the keyboard to play a sprightly melody. Meanwhile, the left hand pounded out a beat, as if the piano were clapping or stamping its feet. In that way, ragtime employed the simultaneous rhythms of African music. Ragtime melodies were syncopated, which means that players accented notes that would not be stressed in much of European music.

The man who made mainstream America go crazy for ragtime, Scott Joplin (1868–1917), studied classical piano as a child in Texarkana, Texas. He was just a teenager in 1885 when he went to St. Louis, Missouri, and found a job playing music at the Silver Dollar Saloon. Pretty soon, word got around that no one in St. Louis could play piano rags as skillfully as Scott Joplin.

In 1899, Joplin wrote and published "Maple Leaf Rag," a piano piece that sold 1 million copies. In no time, black and white Americans were playing ragtime music in towns and cities across the nation. Joplin also wrote an opera, *Treemonisha* (1911), employing African-American music in its varied forms.

The catchy rhythms of ragtime influenced European composers as well. The French composer Claude Debussy included "Golliwog's Cakewalk," a movement with a ragtime beat, in his piano suite *Children's Corner* (1905). Igor Stravinsky, the Russian-born American composer, wrote several works inspired by ragtime, including "Piano-Rag Music" (1920).

Jazz from New Orleans

New Orleans was a musical city at the dawn of the 20th century. Carnivals and parades seemed incomplete without lively music, and there was always a dance being planned. Even a funeral required a band whose dirges escorted the casket from church to graveyard. After the burial, the band changed its tune, and happy, swinging music chased away the mourners' tears.

Many black musicians found steady work in the New Orleans district known as Storyville. This was an unsavory spot that attracted sailors to its honky-tonks and brothels. While most Americans were tapping their feet to ragtime, the music makers of Storyville were cooking up something new. They blended the bent notes of the blues with ragtime's syncopation and created jazz. Improvisation was a key ingredient. The people of the African diaspora had always felt free to play with music, to stretch out notes, alter melodies, or make up lyrics on the spot. Improvisation gave jazz musicians a unique voice. They sang through their instruments, letting loose their feelings and ideas.

Jazz musicians spoke their own language. A *break* was a short, spontaneous solo played in the pause of a song. A *riff* was a musical phrase repeated by band members in a call-and-response pattern. Vocalists joined the jazz conversation by singing *scat,* or improvising with sounds rather than words. With ever-changing breaks, riffs, and scat, a jazz band might play a song many times, but never the same way twice.

In 1917, the U.S. Navy ordered the city of New Orleans to clean up Storyville and close down its night spots. Out-of-work musicians joined the mass of people migrating north. They regrouped in the night clubs and dance halls of northern cities, where they perfected distinctive jazz styles. Chicago-style jazz bands often included saxo-

Trumpet virtuoso Louis Armstrong (The Library of Congress)

phones and high-profile soloists. New York's Harlem was the place to hear jazz piano.

A number of virtuosos, or experts in musical technique, influenced the development of jazz. One of these innovators was trumpeter and vocalist Louis Armstrong (1900–71), who emerged early in the movement and became one of the most famous jazz performers. Armstrong was a brilliant improviser who brought attention to the soloist in jazz performance. As America's "Ambassador of Jazz," he gained worldwide acceptance for black performers. Vocalists left their mark on jazz as well. Billie Holiday (1915–59) and Ella Fitzgerald (1918–96) are two of many celebrated jazz singers.

James P. Johnson (1891–1955) was one of the first people to popularize the jazz piano sound of Harlem. "Men like him. . . could make you sing until your tonsils fell out," commented the singer Ethel Waters. "They stirred you into joy and wild ecstasy. They could make you cry." Johnson's protégé, Thomas "Fats" Waller (1904–43), became one of the most popular jazz performers of all time. Waller wrote numerous songs that have remained favorites among jazz musicians, including "Ain't Misbehavin'" and "Honeysuckle Rose."

Jazz keeps evolving as pioneering musicians explore new sounds and styles. Following the end of World War II, trumpeter John "Dizzy" Gillespie and saxophonist Charlie "Bird" Parker created a new style called bebop. Gillespie (1917–93) tried, he said, to bring jazz back to its roots. He explained that his trumpeting, characterized by short, staccato musical phrases, "reasserted the primacy of rhythm and the blues in our music. . . ."

Another influential jazz trumpeter, Miles Davis (1926–91), was always trying something new. His early combo, the Miles Davis Nonet, featured jazz played on French horns, tubas, and other atypical instruments. In the 1970s, Davis originated the musical style known as fusion, blending elements of rock, soul, and the blues with jazz. At the same time, saxophonist Ornette Coleman, pianist Cecil Taylor, and others were pursuing the experimental style known as free jazz.

Some composers have written orchestral music in a jazz style. Duke Ellington (1899–1974) brought jazz into the world's great concert halls with pieces such as *Black, Brown, and Beige* (1943), inspired by the history of African Americans. The government of Liberia commissioned his *Liberian Suite* in 1947 to mark that country's 100th birthday.

Ellington's music is constructed around solo instrumental performances and sometimes incorporates vocal passages without words. This important American composer is also remembered for the hundreds of songs that he wrote. Some, such as "Sophisticated Lady" and "Mood Indigo," are considered classics of popular music.

Newer Forms and Fashions

African Americans have continued to find new ways to express themselves musically. These range from the uplifting tones of gospel to hard-hitting, message-driven rap.

Gospel music was born in the tents of revival meetings in the early decades of the 20th century, when traveling preachers stirred people up and incited them to sing the Lord's praises. The songs that poured forth had a compelling beat and lyrics full of emotion. People clapped and danced to the music, and they improvised on the melodies, adding harmonies and other embellishments to the traditional spiritual style. Singers called out phrases of song, and the congregation responded.

Gospel music thrived in the Holiness Church, a Pentecostal sect whose members were forbidden to sing for outsiders. But there was no way that one denomination could keep such exciting music to itself. African Americans of all faiths were soon swarming to Holiness churches to hear the gospel sound. Before long, professional gospel singers were making records and touring the country. One of the greatest gospel stars, Mahalia Jackson (1911–72), introduced her music to a worldwide audience. A political activist, Jackson sang at civil rights rallies in the 1950s and 1960s, and she performed at an inauguration party for President John F. Kennedy in 1961.

When gospel vocalists began recording secular (nonreligious) hits in the 1950s, they retained the emotional quality

The Father of Gospel Music _____

In 1921, a blues musician named Georgia Tom Dorsey attended the National Baptist Convention of America. This annual gathering attracted worshipers from all over the country. A high point occurred when the Reverend A. W. Nix stood up to sing. Nix had a powerful voice, and the audience loved his rendition of the gospel song "I Do, Don't You?"

Dorsey listened, and he said to himself, "That's what I'd like to do." From that moment on, Dorsey devoted himself to gospel music. He wrote and published more than 500 religious songs and promoted the careers of other composers and performers. His efforts earned him the title Father of Gospel Music.

Thomas A. Dorsey was born in the small town of Villa Rica, Georgia, in 1899. His father was a traveling preacher who brought the word of God to country churches and revival meetings. Tom's mother played the organ in church, and his uncle wrote hymns. Another uncle "hoboed" from town to town, strumming a guitar and singing. Musical talent seemed to run in the family, and playing the piano came easily to Tom.

Dorsey brought his music to Chicago in 1916, at the start of the Great Migration. "They said it was a place of freedom," he said about Chicago. "I was looking for that." He played in blues joints by night and "demon-

of their singing. Their music, which also drew on the blues and jazz, influenced a new style known as rhythm and blues (R&B). Some rhythm-and-blues artists had a smooth singing style, while others conveyed the raw excitement of a revival meeting. One of the most famous, pianist and singer Ray Charles (born 1930), grew up hearing the blues from cafe jukeboxes and gospel music in church. He has had R&B hits with ballads such as "You Don't Know Me," as well as with fast-paced numbers, including "What'd I Say?," with its gospel-like call-and-response pattern.

In the 1960s, the combination of rhythm-and-blues music with gospel enthusiasm and heavy rhythms produced a new

strated" songs in music stores by day. At that time, a piano in the parlor was the home entertainment center for many families. People often asked a store employee to play a song so that they could hear it before buying the sheet music.

Georgia Tom kept on playing the blues after he started to write gospel music. He toured the United States with Ma Rainey, one of the great early blues singers. Then, in 1929, "the blues ran out," Dorsey said. The Great Depression began, and blues musicians found themselves out of work. Their fans had little money to spare for records or for a night out.

Dorsey took a job directing a church choir and spent his free time writing gospel songs. The inspirations for his songwriting sometimes came from life's troubles. In 1932, Dorsey's wife died in childbirth. Within days, his infant son died as well. Dorsey was devastated. "That was double trouble, and I couldn't take it," he said. Out of his grief he wrote "Precious Lord, Take My Hand," the best-loved gospel song of all time. Its lyrics have been translated into more than 50 languages. That same year, he established Dorsey House of Music to publish the work of black gospel composers. He trained many younger singers in the decades that followed, including Mahalia Jackson.

Thomas A. Dorsey died in 1993. He conveyed the trials and joys of African-American Christians in his songs, and he helped to shape the history of American music.

genre known as soul music. James Brown (born 1933), the electrifying performer known as Soul Brother Number One, had a big hit in 1968 with "Say It Loud, I'm Black and I'm Proud," expressing the new consciousness sweeping the black community. Soul music reached its peak in the art of Aretha Franklin (born 1942), the Queen of Soul, who has had more million-selling records than any other woman in history.

Commenting on the varied forms of music created in the United States, the composer Duke Ellington said, "The common root, of course, comes out of Africa. That's the pulse. The African pulse."

The African pulse beats on in rock and roll, a musical form that originated among black Americans but was largely taken over by whites. The same pulse drives rap, a form of musical expression invented in America's inner cities during the late 1970s. Rap artists employ a highly developed vocal style that highlights the rhythmic delivery of lyrics and sophisticated rhymes. Rap songs often are political protests or convey the hard realities of city life.

Whatever their chosen form of expression, young African-American performers and song writers pay homage to their musical forebears. Guitarist Ben Harper (born 1970) plays original compositions on antique instruments. His influences include early blues recordings and the gospel music his family likes to hear. He has said, "You feel your ancestral heritage, whether you're conscious of it or not and whether you act upon it or not. I feel it strongly. It's a large part of my expression."

Music of the Diaspora

People throughout the African diaspora find musical inspiration in their ancestral heritage. In Venezuela, the word *golpe*, which means "beat," refers to several musical forms that exhibit African patterns of drumming. Calypso music resulted when Trinidadians blended African and European musical elements in the late 19th century. Words dominate melody in calypso, as they do in rap. Calypso singers play with words, stressing unaccented syllables and creating clever rhymes. They often act as town criers, singing about the latest scandal or sporting match.

In places such as Salvador, Brazil, a seacoast city whose population is mostly black, bands of street musicians play *axe* (pronounced ah-SHAY), rhythmic music with raplike lyrics that are recited rather than sung. Some axe groups urge

A *demonstration of* Haitian *drumming and dancing at the* 1944 National Folk Festival in Philadelphia (The Library of Congress)

people to stand up to racism and take pride in their blackness, as the soul artists of the 1960s did.

Music is closely tied to dance in South America and the Caribbean nations. The Angolan word *semba,* meaning "invitation to dance," became *samba,* the name of a popular Brazilian dance and the music that accompanies it. The samba began as a folk dance performed in a circle. People moved to highly syncopated music dominated by percussion instruments and call-and-response vocals. With the ending of slavery in the 19th century and black migration to Brazil's cities, the samba became a dance for couples that was suitable for urban night spots. Samba music, like jazz, has inspired instrumentalists to improvise and experiment.

The samba gained international popularity in the 1920s and 1930s, along with an African-inspired Cuban dance, the rumba. Afro-Cubans danced the rumba at festivals while beating out rhythms with pots and spoons, rattles and drums —or anything else that came to hand.

Electric instruments provide the sound for reggae, a form of music that originated in Jamaica in the 1960s. A loud electric bass is the lead instrument in a traditional reggae band. Electric lead and rhythm guitars, an organ, a piano, and drums round out the ensemble. Reggae music is known for its unique rhythm pattern of alternating tension and release. Its lyrics tend to reflect the social concerns of the poor and the teachings of the Jamaican Rastafarian movement, most notably the deity of Emperor Haile Selassie of Ethiopia.

Dance in the United States

Like the samba and the rumba, much social dance in the United States is more African than European. From the Charleston of the 1920s through the jitterbug of the 1940s, the twist of the 1960s, and the dance moves popular today, dances originating in the black community have taken hold in the larger population.

Tap dance is an art form created by African Americans. It is thought to have begun during the time of slavery, when people who were forbidden to drum tapped out rhythms with their feet. Tap dancing caught the public's attention at the start of the 20th century. It reached its height of popularity in the 1930s, when tap dancers were featured in musical motion pictures.

Several outstanding dancers have contributed to the development of tap. They include Bill "Bojangles" Robinson (1878–1949), famed for the rhythmic complexity of his dancing. Modern audiences remember Robinson best for his appearance in the 1935 film *The Little Colonel* with Shirley Temple. John W. Bubbles (1902–86) had an energetic dancing style. In 1935, he was in the original cast of *Porgy and*

Bess, George Gershwin's opera set among the African Americans of the South Carolina coast. The most celebrated contemporary tap dancer is Gregory Hines (born 1946). Hines performed in the 1978 musical play *Eubie!,* a tribute to composer Eubie Blake. His films include *The Cotton Club* (1984) and *White Nights* (1985), in which he performed with the Russian-American ballet dancer Mikhail Baryshnikov. Hines is strongly interested in the history of tap and participated in the 1989 television documentary *Tappin': The Making of Tap.*

Black professional dancers have enriched their art by researching its Africanness. Katherine Dunham (born 1909), one of the most important choreographers of the 20th century, studied anthropology as a young woman. Her work brought her to Haiti, Jamaica, Trinidad, and Martinique as she sought the African origins of Caribbean dance. Dunham demonstrated that African rites and dances serve as a framework for West Indian social and cultural life. From the 1930s through the 1950s, her dance company toured the world, introducing audiences to the dance of Africa and the African diaspora. Dunham counsels black dancers to remember their ancestry. "It's very easy to lose your balance and equilibrium in the world today," she has stated. "The drum was meant to hold us together—and it does." Contemporary Dunham disciples include Chuck Davis and Charles Moore, both of whom have founded influential companies that explore African dance traditions.

Sculpture and Painting

During the 18th and 19th centuries, black artists had to paint like Europeans if they were to have successful careers. They had to follow the rules of perspective and create traditional portraits and landscapes. Most of the New Englanders who admired the paintings of Edward Bannister (1828–1901) had no idea that the artist was an African American. Robert Scott Duncanson (1821–72), who achieved success as a landscape artist on the western frontier, influenced the Hudson River school of painting. Edmonia Lewis (c. 1843–after 1911) was the first professional African-American sculptor. She settled in Rome, where she felt free to explore her African-American and Native American roots through art.

Henry Ossawa Tanner (1859–1937) was one of the first black artists who painted African-American subjects in a true-to-life way. One of his most famous works, *The Banjo Lesson,* portrays an old black man teaching a boy to play the banjo. It symbolizes the passing of African-American culture from one generation to the next.

Bible stories inspired Tanner as well. He likened African Americans' struggle against racism to the persecution of the early Christians. His painting *The Raising of Lazarus* earned him a prestigious medal from the Paris Salon of 1896.

Early in the 20th century, African masks and carved figures inspired Pablo Picasso and other European artists to experiment with cubism and abstraction. Suddenly, African art was fashionable in the center of the art world. African-American artists such as Meta Warrick Fuller (1877–1968) hurried to Paris, where they could explore their artistic heritage in an atmosphere free of prejudice.

Fuller lived overseas from 1900 until 1902. She continued her study of sculpture after returning to the United States, and in 1914, she completed *Ethiopia Awakening,* a piece that foreshadowed the Harlem Ren-

Let's bare our arms and plunge them deep through laughter, through pain, through sorrow, through hope, through disappointment, into the very depths of the souls of our people and drag forth material crude, rough, neglected. Then let's sing it, dance it, write it, paint it.

—Aaron Douglas in a letter to Langston Hughes (December 21, 1925)

Augusta Savage prepares clay models for her sculpture Lift Ev'ry Voice and Sing (Photographs and Prints Division, Schomburg Center for Research in Black Culture, The New York Public Library, Astor, Lenox and Tilden Foudations)

aissance. The statue depicts an African woman partially covered in a mummy's wrappings and coming to life after centuries of sleep.

Fuller never lived in Harlem, but Aaron Douglas (1899–1979) flourished there. Inspired by the African art he viewed in museums and the jazz he heard in Harlem night-clubs, he pioneered an abstract, geometric painting style that ignored Western rules of perspective. Like an ancient Egyptian artist decorating the walls of a temple, he painted flat figures, without depth, standing with their heads in profile. In the 1930s, Douglas painted four murals for Countee Cullen Branch of the New York Public Library. They depict scenes from African-American history, ranging from an idyllic African past to life in a northern U.S. city. His murals also decorate the library at Fisk University in Nashville, Tennessee.

Palmer Hayden (1890–1973), another artist of the Harlem Renaissance, painted scenes of everyday black life. He deliberately employed the style of an unschooled folk artist who might exaggerate human features in an attempt to render his subject honestly. In 1944, Hayden began a major project, a series of 12 paintings on the life of John Henry, a mythic railroad worker praised in story and song by black Americans.

The sculptor Augusta Savage (1892–1962) chose real human heroes as her subjects. She created busts of W. E. B. Du Bois, Marcus Garvey, and other notable African Americans. In 1937, the New York World's Fair commissioned Savage to sculpt a work celebrating African-American contributions to music. Inspired by James Weldon Johnson's lyrics to the classic song "Lift Ev'ry Voice and Sing," she fashioned an enormous harp with each string emanating from a singing black child.

Younger Generations of Artists

In 1938, Savage helped a 21-year-old painter named Jacob Lawrence find steady employment with the Works Progress Administration (WPA). This government agency put people to work during the Great Depression of the 1930s. The WPA paid Lawrence a weekly salary to paint pictures. The job allowed him to perfect his technique and become an important 20th-century artist.

Lawrence paints in an abstract, angular style. He finds his subjects in African-American history and everyday life. He often creates series of paintings, such as his 41 panels on the life of Toussaint Louverture, the father of Haitian independence. Another series presents scenes from the Great Migration. In the 1950s, Lawrence undertook his most ambitious series, *Struggle: From the History of the American People,* in which he expanded his view to include Americans of all races. In 1970, the National Association for the Advancement of Colored People (NAACP) honored Lawrence with its Spingarn Medal, awarded to African Americans of accomplishment. Lawrence said in his acceptance speech, "If I have achieved a degree of success as a creative artist, it is mainly due to the black experience which is our heritage— an experience which gives inspiration, motivation, and stimulation."

Today's African-American artists draw on that heritage in a variety of ways. Sam Gilliam (born 1933) is a prominent painter who proves that even nonrepresentational art— works that are completely abstract, that depict no recognizable scenes, objects, or figures—can be rooted in African-American culture. The jazz of Miles Davis and other black musicians inspired Gilliam to create geometric collages in the 1970s. He also has made "quilted" paintings by cutting up thickly painted canvases and arranging the pieces in patterns. The results remind him of quilts made by African-American women that he saw as a child.

Keith Morrison (born 1942) fills his paintings with all kinds of fantastic figures: imaginary animals, supernatural beings, and people in African masks. Morrison, who was born in Jamaica and educated in the United States, draws on African and Caribbean lore in paintings such as *Zombie Jamboree* (1968), which combines sinister magical imagery with bright tropical colors. Morrison hopes that his work will bring the peoples of Africa, Europe, Asia, and the Americas closer together. He looks forward to "a true world culture of ideas in the Twenty First Century."

NOTES

p. 79   "a lean, loose-jointed Negro . . ." W. C. Handy, *Father of the Blues* (New York: Macmillan Co., 1941), p. 74.

p. 79   "the weirdest music I ever heard." Handy, p. 74.

p. 80   "the stuff the people wanted . . ." Handy, p. 77.

p. 80   "Southern Negroes sang . . ." Handy, p. 74.

p. 84   "Men like him . . ." Ethel Waters with Charles Samuels, *His Eye Is on the Sparrow* (New York: Doubleday & Co., 1951), p. 145.

p. 84   "reasserted the primacy . . ." Dizzy Gillespie with Al Fraser, *To Be or Not . . . to Bop* (New York: Doubleday, 1979), p. 369.

p. 86   "That's what I'd like to do." Quoted in Jim O'Neal and Amy O'Neal, "Living Blues Interview: Georgia Tom Dorsey," *Living Blues* (May 1975), p. 29

p. 86   "They said it was . . ." Quoted in O'Neal and O'Neal, p. 19.

p. 87   "the blues ran out." Quoted in O'Neal and O'Neal, p. 28.

p. 87   "That was double trouble . . ." Thomas A. Dorsey, "Precious Lord," *Decision* (December 1974), p. 4.

p. 87   "The common root, of course . . ." Quoted in Columbus Salley, *The Black 100* (New York: Citadel Press, 1993), p. 242.

p. 88   "You feel your ancestral heritage . . ." Quoted in Jas Obrecht, "'I Want to Be Ready': Ben Harper Plays in Praise of Jah," *Guitar Player* (September 1997), p. 41.

p. 91   "It's very easy . . ." Quoted in Esther Iverem, "Bridges from Past to Future," *Washington Post,* July 6, 1996, p. C5.

p. 92   "Let's bare our arms . . ." Quoted in Amy Helene Kirschke, *Aaron Douglas: Art, Race, and the Harlem Renaissance* (Jackson, Miss.: University Press of Mississippi, 1995), pp. 79–80.

p. 95   "If I have achieved . . ." Jacob Lawrence, "The Artist Responds," *The Crisis* (August/September 1970), p. 266.

p. 95   "a true world culture . . ." Quoted in Regenia A. Perry, *Free Within Ourselves: African-American Artists in the Collection of the National Museum of American Art* (Washington, D.C.: National Museum of American Art, Smithsonian Institution, 1992), p. 147.

7

Singular Eloquence
Religion in the African Diaspora

From the time of their arrival in the New World, African Americans have preserved their individuality and maintained a link with the past through religion. Belief in God has been a creative force within the black populations of the Western Hemisphere. The result is a variety of faiths in which people preach, pray, sing, and give thanks much as their forebears did.

In the United States, the church has long been a center of political activity in the black community. Nineteenth-century African-American ministers were among the most outspoken abolitionists, and their congregations sheltered people who were escaping slavery on the Underground Railroad. Martin Luther King Jr., Ralph Abernathy, and other civil rights leaders of the 1950s and 1960s were ordained ministers who preached a "social gospel." They transformed their faith into nonviolent political action for the benefit of society. Much of the social and legal progress achieved during those decades would have been impossible without the black clergy as an organizing and driving force.

Churches also have provided economic, social, and educational aid. The writer and sociologist W. E. B. Du Bois listed the many benefits that one African-American congregation gained from its church in 1903: "Various organizations meet here—the church proper, the Sunday-school, two or three insurance societies, women's socie-ties, and mass meetings of various kinds. Entertainments, suppers, and lectures are held beside the five or six regular weekly services. Considerable sums of money are collected and expended here, employment is found for the idle, strangers are introduced, news disseminated, and charity distributed." Today, even churches in poor communities offer day care, tutoring, job placement, and cultural en-richment for their members.

Two factors contributed to the rise of African-American churches in the United States: the prejudice that people encountered in traditionally white houses of worship and the desire for autonomy in religious life. Thus, out of necessity and by choice, African Americans formed their own faiths and fellowships. They have made the black church the most authentically African-American institu-tion in modern society.

The Role of Folk Churches

Black churches sprang up across the South after the Civil War. In small "folk" churches, country people nurtured a close, personal relationship with the divine. They sought God's message in dreams and visions. Prayer was vocal, emotional, and musical. Pastors delivered stirring sermons, often singing or chanting their messages, while congregations called out responses.

But the need to worship freely and equally was not unique to the postwar South. Early in the 19th century, African Americans in a northern city established a major Protestant denomination.

The history of that denomination began in 1787, when a black Methodist minister named Richard Allen attended a Methodist service in Philadelphia. A church official interrupted Allen's prayer and told him to move to a section reserved for African Americans. Allen walked out rather than submit to segregation, and the other black worshipers followed him. "And they were no more plagued with us in the church," Allen wrote.

Allen never forgot the incident. In 1816, he and other concerned African Americans founded the African Methodist Episcopal Church, with Allen as its first bishop. Today, more than 3 million people belong to the AME Church, which is also represented in Africa, England, Canada, and the West Indies. The church sponsors schools and colleges, including Wilberforce University in Ohio and the Monrovia College and Industrial Training School in Liberia.

The AME Church feels a strong responsibility to minister to African Americans, yet it welcomes members of all races. The church accepts the basic Methodist teachings of Christian perfection and personal salvation through faith.

> The black and massive form of the preacher swayed and quivered as the words crowded to his lips and flew at us in singular eloquence. The people moaned and fluttered, and then the gaunt-cheeked brown woman beside me suddenly leaped straight into the air and shrieked like a lost soul, while round about came wail and groan and outcry, and a scene of human passion such as I had never conceived before.
>
> ◆
>
> —W. E. B. Du Bois, *The Souls of Black Folk* (1903)

Another Methodist organization, the African Methodist Episcopal Zion Church, also claims many members. It was the church of Harriet Tubman, Frederick Douglass, and Sojourner Truth, and so it has a proud history.

The predominant religious groups among African Americans, however, are the Baptist churches. More than 7 million people belong to the National Baptist Convention, U.S.A. (NBCUSA), founded in Atlanta in 1895. The National Baptist Convention of America, Inc. (NBCA), which split from the NBCUSA in 1915, may have as many as 5 million members. The African-American population supports several other Baptist conventions as well. The National Baptist Publishing Board, Inc., founded in Nashville in 1896, ranks as the world's largest black-owned religious publisher. Baptists regard the Bible as the ultimate authority in matters of religious belief and custom. They practice baptism by immersion as a public confession of faith.

Religious Diversity

The rural people who migrated to northern cities in the 20th century discovered religious options that were unavailable in the South. While many joined large, established Protestant churches, others found different ways to worship. The Roman Catholic Church saw a pronounced increase in black membership. Some African Americans converted to tradi-

Young Chicagoans attend a Roman Catholic mass in March 1942. (The Library of Congress)

tional forms of Judaism or Islam. Many people raised in folk congregations of the South felt most at ease in the storefront churches of the Pentecostal, Holiness, and Black Spiritual sects. Some followed charismatic leaders such as Father Divine, who became a figure of national importance during the 1930s. "The Black community, by the end of the decade of the 1930s, was literally glutted with churches of every variety and description," writes Gayraud S. Wilmore, an authority on African-American religion.

Several religious movements arose from the desire to find a historical origin for the people of sub-Saharan Africa. In 1896, a man named William S. Crowdy formed the Church of God and Saints of Christ in Lawrence, Kansas. Despite the church's name, it was founded on Jewish teachings. Crowdy professed that the original Africans were the lost tribes of Israel, who were taken from their homeland by the Assyrians in the eighth century B.C.

The Commandment Keepers of the Living God was another assembly based on Judaism. Established in Harlem in the 1920s with West Indian immigrants as its first members, the Commandment Keepers taught that African Americans

Photographer Gordon Parks captured a woman's intense joy upon receiving a blessing at St. Martin's Spiritual Church, Washington, D.C. (The Library of Congress)

descended from Ethiopian Jews and that slavery had robbed them of their Jewish faith.

Starting in 1913, African Americans belonging to the Moorish Science Temple in Newark, New Jersey, practiced Islam in the belief that their ancestors came from Morocco, an Islamic country. But the dominant black Islamic group—and an important religious and political force in 20th-century America—began in Detroit in 1930. In that year a peddler named W. D. Fard founded the Nation of Islam.

Fard preached that African Americans were actually Muslims, members of a "lost-found tribe of Shabazz." He advocated racial pride, solidarity, and self-reliance. In four years, he built a temple and schools and started a paramilitary force.

Elijah Muhammad succeeded Fard as head of the Nation of Islam (also known as the Black Muslims) in 1934. Under his guidance, the organization built 80 temples and attracted thousands of converts, including Malcolm X, who became a leading spokesman for the group. Stressing economic independence for African Americans, the Nation of Islam opened restaurants, stores, and laundries in many cities. The group raised produce and livestock on farms and imported fish from Peru. In the 1970s, the Nation of Islam's newspaper, *Muhammad Speaks,* had a circulation of 600,000.

The organization split after Elijah Muhammad's death in 1975. His son, Warith Deen Muhammad, led the majority of Black Muslims toward observance of traditional Islam. Louis Farrakhan emerged as the controversial head of a more radical and politically oriented organization, also called the Nation of Islam. Farrakhan has been criticized for inspiring hatred of whites, especially Jews. He also has been praised for his efforts to combat the social problems that African Americans face, particularly in inner-city neighborhoods. Farrakhan organized the Million Man March of October

Customers shop at Your Supermarket, owned and operated by the Nation of Islam, in 1970. The apples offered for sale were grown on Nation of Islam orchards. (The Library of Congress)

1995, in which hundreds of thousands of African-American men gathered in Washington, D.C., to commit themselves to family and community.

African-Based Religions of the Diaspora

Africanisms are evident in religions that have developed in Haiti, Brazil, Cuba, and other countries with large black populations. These religions combine the rituals and belief systems of Africans, European Christians, and sometimes Indians. Practitioners often attend Catholic or Protestant churches as well.

The African-based religion known as Vodou, or Voodoo, originated among enslaved workers on Haitian sugar plantations in the 18th century. The word *vodou* derives from the Fon language of Dahomey (present-day Benin) and refers to the gods *(vodun)* that govern people's lives and control the forces of nature. In Haiti, enslaved Africans borrowed rites from Roman Catholicism, which was the faith of the colony's French rulers, and wove them into their traditional belief pattern. They equated many gods of their homeland with Catholic saints. For example, they saw similarities between the Dahomeyan serpent god, Da, and St. Patrick, who rid Ireland of snakes, according to legend.

Belief in a supreme being, or *Bon Dieu*, is at the core of Vodou. As in Catholicism, worship involves crucifixes, baptism, confession, and communion. Vodou is African in its reliance on dancing and drumming, and in it emphasis on spirit possession. Priests enter a trance, or altered state of consciousness, in which spirits inhabit their bodies in order to perform cures or give advice. Vodou has followers in Cuba, Trinidad, Brazil, and the southern United States as well as in Haiti.

The enslaved Africans of Brazil melded traditional beliefs with Catholicism and Indian rituals to create regional religions that continue to flourish. In the Bantu-influenced Macumba faith of Rio de Janeiro, the ghosts of African ancestors take possession of worshipers. Candomblé, practiced in the predominantly black Bahia region, involves sacrifice, drumming, song, and possession. The faithful perform

The Imani Temple

On the morning of July 9, 1989, 2,000 people crowded a Suitland, Maryland, high school auditorium. They were African-American Roman Catholics from the Washington, D.C., area. They had come to worship this Sunday with the Reverend George A. Stallings Jr., a Catholic priest who had broken away from the church to found the independent Imani Temple. (*Imani* is the Swahili word for "faith.") Wearing a robe of African design, Stallings shouted to be heard over the music of drums and bells. He said, "If you're happy and you know it say 'Amen!'" The faithful called out, "Amen!"

The desire to tailor Catholicism to African-American needs had led Stallings to defy church leadership. In 1974, he was a newly ordained priest assigned to St. Teresa of Avila Church in an African-American section of Washington, D.C. Like some other Catholic churches that serve black populations, St. Teresa of Avila offered the Gospel Mass, a Catholic mass that incorporated the song, dance, clapping, and vocal call and response of traditional black Protestant services.

Soon, Stallings was urging the church to do more for its African-American members. There were some 2 million black Catholics in the country but fewer than 300 black priests. Many African-American par-

dances learned from Brazilian Indians in which they move in a circle and shuffle their feet.

Jamaican Revivalism borrowed from the Baptist Church. The spirits that possess people at Revivalist meetings are biblical figures. They include the prophets of the Old Testament, the apostles of the Gospels, and the Holy Ghost. The music of Revivalism takes its tunes and lyrics from Protestant hymns and its rhythmic drumming from Africa.

Burial customs are important in the Afro-Christian religions of the diaspora, just as they were in West Africa. Some Brazilian sects conduct a weeklong ritual known as *acheche*, during which they ask the spirits of their ancestors to wel-

ishes were served by white priests who lacked the skills and knowledge needed to address the problems of black families and youth. In 1988, Cardinal James Hickey responded by creating a new position for Father Stallings, appointing him evangelist on behalf of the black community. But Stallings was even more critical of the church in his new role, and he left the following year.

Not all African-American Catholics approved of the Imani Temple. According to Bishop John Ricard of Baltimore, Stallings's action "obscures the authentic aspirations of African American Catholics as they seek not to sever ties with our church but to enrich it with the unique gifts the African American experience can bring." Many, however, applauded Stallings. "The church has to come to understand more and more that we have a need to exercise and focus on our own culture," stated Walter Hubbard, executive director of the National Office for Black Catholics in Atlanta.

The publicity he received helped Stallings establish more congregations in neighboring states. In 1990, he was consecrated as a bishop in the American National Catholic Church, which was formed in the 19th century and rejects certain Roman Catholic teachings. The Imani Temple congregation accepted this new allegiance, and now, meeting in their own Washington, D.C., church, they carry on Stallings's mission of social activism in the black community.

come the newly deceased. Jamaican Revivalists believe that a dead person's spirit, called a duppy, returns on the ninth night after death to possess the body of a religious leader. The duppy uses this occasion to bequeath his or her worldly goods or, in cases of murder, to identify the killer. A duppy can cause misfortune for survivors if his or her funeral was carried out improperly.

Santería

More black Cubans trace their ancestry to the Yoruba than to any other African ethnic group, and the Afro-Cuban religion Santería has its origins in Yoruban society. Practitioners of Santería worship a creator known as Oloddumare. They identify the traditional Yoruban deities, which are called *orishas,* or sometimes *orisas,* with the saints of the Catholic Church. During the years of slavery in Cuba, the trappings of Catholicism masked Yoruban rituals, which were forbidden. One former Cuban slave recalled how the Spanish overseers were fooled: "They would make some remark in passing like, 'What's going on here?', and the Negroes would say, 'We're celebrating San Juan [St. John].' But of course it was not San Juan but Oggun, the god of war . . . ."

In Santería today, Oggun and the other orishas act as guides and protectors of humankind. Each believer petitions only one orisha, which acts as his or her guardian. The faithful wear necklaces of colored beads corresponding to the most powerful orishas. Red and white beads are for Shango, the thunder god; blue and white represent Yamaya, goddess of the seas; and yellow is for Oshun, the goddess of fresh water. Divination is central to the practice of Santería. The priests of Santería, called *santeros,* use cowrie shells, coconut rinds, and divining boards to communicate with the orishas.

> The basic difference between the Yoruba priest and the santero is that the latter practices his magic in the asphalt jungles of the big cities instead of the African wilderness.
>
> ◆
>
> Migene González-Wippler, *Santería: The Religion* (1989)

Santería gained official acceptance when Cuba achieved independence in 1902. But since 1959, the government of Fidel Castro has suppressed the religion, calling it a divisive force in society. Practitioners of Santería have been among the thousands of refugees fleeing Cuba for the United States. They now worship openly in Miami, New York, and other American cities, where *botánicas,* or specialty shops, sell the objects used in prayer and divination. Black and white Americans, in small but growing numbers, are converting to Santería. There are Yoruba-based religious communities today in Brazil, Cuba, the United States, and, of course, Nigeria. They have formed an international organization, the Orisa Tradition, which began holding yearly conferences in the 1980s. The Orisa Tradition is one way in which the people of the diaspora have renewed ties with the continent of Africa.

NOTES

p. 98   "Various organizations meet here . . ." W. E. B. Du Bois, *The Souls of Black Folk* (1903; New York: Bantam Books, 1989), p. 136.

p. 99   "The black and massive . . ." Du Bois, *The Souls of Black Folk,* p. 134.

p. 99   "And they were no . . ." Richard Allen, "Life Experience and Gospel Labors," in Milton C. Sernett, ed., *Afro-American Religious History* (Durham, N.C.: Duke University Press, 1985), p. 142.

p. 100   "A sign on the outside . . ." Benjamin E. Mays and Joseph W. Nicholson, *The Negro's Church* (New York: Institute of Social and Religious Research, 1933), p. 283.

p. 101   "The Black community . . ." Gayraud S. Wilmore, *Black Religion and Black Radicalism: An Interpretation of the Religious History of Afro-American People* (Maryknoll, N.Y.: Orbis Books, 1983), p. 222.

p. 106   "If you're happy . . ." Quoted in Marjorie Hyer, "'Ain't No Stopping Us Now,' Stallings Exults," *Washington Post,* July 10, 1989, p. D1.

p. 107   "obscures the authentic aspirations . . ." Quoted in Marjorie Hyer, "Hickey Criticizes Priest's Plan for Black Catholic Church," *Washington Post,* June 21, 1989, p. C1.

p. 107   "The church has to come . . ." Quoted in Daniel Moamah-Wiafe, *The Black Experience in Contemporary America* (2d ed.; Omaha, Neb.: BW Wisdom Publications, 1993), p. 157.

p. 108 "They would make some remark . . ." Esteban Montejo, *The Autobiography of a Runaway Slave,* Miguel Barnet, ed., Jocasta Innes, trans. (London: The Bodley Head, 1968), p. 80

p. 108 "The basic difference . . ." Migene González-Wippler, *Santería: The Religion* (New York: Harmony Books, 1989), p. 18.

8

Bright Star

Reaching Back to Africa

From the time of the Middle Passage, when prisoners dreamed of rebirth in Africa, the people of the African diaspora have felt a longing for their homeland. They began renewing their ties with Africa as early as the late 18th century. In 1787, British abolitionists established a colony at Freetown, Sierra Leone, as a haven for former slaves from the West Indies and the United States. An African-American shipbuilder and seaman named Paul Cuffee transported 38 free blacks from Massachusetts to Sierra Leone in 1815.

Many whites favored repatriation, or the return of blacks to Africa, for reasons ranging from compassion to prejudice. Witnessing how free blacks endured discrimination and hardship, some whites concluded that African Americans would never achieve equality in the United States. A better life had to await them in Africa. Others, including Thomas Jefferson, advocated a return to Africa because they were repelled by the idea of an integrated society. There were also whites who hoped that repatriated blacks would bring Christianity and "civilization" to Africa.

The American Colonization Society

A group of whites formed the American Colonization Society in 1816, with the goal of establishing a colony in Africa for African Americans. In 1822, the society began clearing land at Cape Mesurado on the West Coast of Africa. The settlement built there, Monrovia, was the first town in the colony of Liberia.

The people pictured in this 19th-century magazine illustration traveled from Arkansas to New York City in the hope of immigrating to Liberia. They have been given shelter at a Baptist church while they await passage. (The Library of Congress)

Until it stopped operation in 1865, the society sent 147 ships with 18,959 settlers to Liberia. Most were free African Americans who emigrated voluntarily. A smaller number were enslaved persons whose owners paid for their passage to Africa because they were old or unproductive, or as a reward for loyal service.

The settlers put ashore in a land with dense tropical forests and a severe climate. Long dry spells alternated with months of heavy rain. Infectious diseases were rampant, and doctors were in short supply. It is no surprise that many people died of tropical fevers. War was another problem. Sixteen distinct ethnic groups already lived in the region, and at times they clashed with the newcomers. But settlement persisted in spite of the hardships, and Liberia became an independent nation in 1847, pledging to "provide a home for the dispersed children of Africa."

While some African Americans welcomed the chance to start a new life in Africa, most black leaders denounced the practice of repatriation—especially when it was controlled by whites. "Shame upon the guilty wretches that dare propose, and all that countenance such a proposition," wrote Frederick Douglass in the antislavery newspaper the *North Star.* "We live here—have lived here —have a right to live here, and mean to live here." The abolitionist Henry Highland Garnet agreed, stating, "We are planted here."

Dr. Martin R. Delany was one prominent African American who favored colonization in Africa. He observed that his people were already enduring "disappointment, discouragement, and degradation"; life in Africa could hardly be worse. In May

> We love this country and its liberties, if we could share an equal right in them; but our freedom is partial, and we have no hope that it will ever be otherwise here; therefore we had rather be gone, though we should suffer hunger and nakedness for years.
>
> ◆
>
> —Abraham Camp, a free African American, in a letter to the American Colonization Society (1818)

1859, Delany left the United States to spend a year exploring the Niger River valley of Africa and negotiating to buy land for black resettlement. He abandoned the project in 1861, at the start of the Civil War, and counseled African Americans to remain in the United States and support the northern cause. Foreseeing that a Union victory in the war would bring an end to slavery, he enlisted as an officer with an African-American regiment. He rose quickly to the rank of major.

But even after emancipation, Africa remained appealing. Benjamin "Pap" Singleton, the visionary who brought thousands of African Americans to Kansas, formed the United Transatlantic Society in 1885. This organization intended to create a nation in Africa, but it never sent anyone overseas. Dr. J. Albert Thorne, a physician and native of Barbados, tried to purchase land in central Africa as a haven for West Indian and American blacks. Although he promoted his plan from the 1890s through the 1920s, Thorne never amassed enough capital to make it a success.

One African People

African Americans grow up with a "double consciousness," wrote W. E. B. Du Bois in 1903. "One ever feels his twoness, —an American, a Negro; two souls, two thoughts, two unreconciled strivings. . . ." Du Bois said that while one part of this consciousness strives to be accepted by white society, the other—the Negro, or black aspect—pulls in another direction, toward unity with all descendants of Africa.

In 1899, a Trinidadian lawyer named Henry Sylvester Williams coined the word *pan-Africanism* to describe the unity of African peoples everywhere. Du Bois adopted the term and made pan-Africanism a key concept in his writing. His own definition came to include the struggle of all black people against white oppression. He viewed the efforts to free Africa from European colonization and to gain equality in the United States as parts of the same problem.

Du Bois and other black intellectuals were alarmed at European domination of Africa. In 1884, several European nations and the United States had sent delegates to a conference in Berlin, Germany. The delegates carved up the map of Africa, outlining their spheres of influence. They wrote rules for the occupation of the African coasts and for navigation on the Congo and Niger Rivers. No African states were invited to the conference. By the end of the century, virtually all of Africa was under European control.

In 1900, Du Bois and representatives of African and New World nations discussed their concerns in London, England, at the Pan-African Congress. Du Bois organized five more such congresses between 1919 and 1945 to draw attention to issues that affected black people everywhere.

Marcus Garvey

Du Bois's message had its greatest resonance among educated and prosperous African Americans. Many more black Americans—especially the working-class newcomers to northern cities—responded to the words of Marcus Garvey.

Born in Jamaica in 1887, the grandson of enslaved Africans, Garvey brought his rallying cry of black pride and solidarity to the United States in 1916. "Wake up Ethiopia! Wake up Africa!" Garvey urged. "Let us work toward the one glorious end of a free, redeemed and mighty nation. Let Africa be a bright star among the constellation of nations."

Garvey's organization, the Universal Negro Improvement Association (UNIA), worked to advance all black people economically through the establishment of black-run businesses. The UNIA also created the Black Star Steamship Line to transport blacks to Africa and to facilitate trade between

Marcus Garvey posed in a photographer's studio wearing his full-dress uniform.
(The Library of Congress)

Africa and the nations of the diaspora. The UNIA had as many as 4 million members at its peak and more than 30 branches. Offices opened in Nigeria in 1920 and in South Africa in 1921.

Nineteen twenty-one was also the year when Garvey declared himself provisional president of the Empire of Africa. He wore an ornate uniform and held conferences to discuss Africa's future. He unsuccessfully petitioned the League of Nations to turn over former German colonies in Africa to the UNIA.

Garvey's influence was widespread. Kwame Nkrumah (1909–72), the first president of Ghana, credited Garvey with awakening his own nationalistic feelings. The idealistic Jamaican also inspired Kenya's first president, Jomo Kenyatta (1891?–1978). However, Garvey's influence declined sharply after 1925, when he was jailed for fraudulent use of the U.S. mails in connection with the Black Star Line. After serving two years, Garvey was deported as an undesirable alien and returned to Jamaica as a national hero. He moved to England in 1935 and continued to advocate pan-African ideas until his death in 1940.

Interest in African settlement declined in the 1930s, although some prominent black Americans have gone to live in Africa. In 1961, at the age of 92, W. E. B. Du Bois was so disillusioned with U.S. democracy that he emigrated to Ghana. Stokely Carmichael, a major figure in the civil rights movement during the 1960s, moved to Guinea in 1969 and adopted the name Kwame Ture. Individuals from diverse fields, including writer Maya Angelou and astronaut Mae Jemison, have lived for a time in Africa.

To Educate and Enlighten

American missionary societies directed their efforts overseas at the start of the 19th century, when African-American churches especially felt the need to serve the people of Africa, to bring them schools and health care along with Christian teaching.

An African Methodist Episcopal (AME) missionary named Daniel Coker sailed on the first ship carrying immigrants to Liberia in 1820. Other black missionaries followed, and by 1886 the AME Church was firmly established in Liberia and Sierra Leone. Representatives of other denominations went to Africa as well. One of the best known was John Small, a bishop of the African Methodist Episcopal Zion (AMEZ) Church. Born in Barbados, Small first went to Africa in 1863. He learned several African languages and studied the needs and customs of the native people. He founded a school in the Gold Coast (present-day Ghana) and helped promising young Africans gain admission to Livingstone College, an AMEZ institution in the United States.

Some 600 African-American missionaries have gone to Africa since 1820. They represent a tiny fraction of the 350,000 Americans who have served their churches on the African continent, but they have been a significant link between African Americans and the people of their ancestral homeland.

Like the black churches, African-American schools have sought to befriend Africans and better their lives. Booker T. Washington attracted African students to the Tuskegee Institute in the early 20th century, promising that the knowledge they gained would aid in the development of their countries. Washington encouraged Tuskegee's American-born students to study their African heritage, and he sent some of his graduates overseas as technical advisers to African governments. Today, a number of American and African colleges take part in cooperative ventures. For example, the University of Maryland, Eastern Shore, shares knowledge and programs with Zambia University. Every year, Clark Atlanta University invites representatives of African and Caribbean nations to discuss topics of mutual concern.

Secrets in the Soil

Another way to reconnect with Africa is to look into the past. Since the late 1960s, archaeologists have been excavating the sites of slave cabins in the South. The cabins were torn down long ago, but many of the inhabitants' belongings remain in the earth. The artifacts include possessions transported from Africa, things the slaves made themselves, and items produced by whites and adapted by the enslaved people for their own use. Studying these objects yields clues about the African heritage of the enslaved people and their contribution to American culture.

Archaeological digs in Colonial Williamsburg, at plantations along the James River in Virginia, and at the homes of presidents George Washington, Thomas Jefferson, and Andrew Jackson have added to our understanding of the daily lives of enslaved African Americans. They shed light on an aspect of history overlooked in written accounts from the period.

The conditions under which Africans traveled to the New World made it all but impossible to bring possessions from home. Therefore, anything that came to America aboard the ships of the Middle Passage must have been highly valued by its owner and may have been handed down from one generation to the next. Archaeologists have found only a few objects that can be traced to Africa on the sites of slave dwellings. Among them are three cowrie shells, which were used in Africa as money or for divination. An ebony bead was unearthed from an old trash pit on a James River plantation. (Ebony is the hard black wood of an African tree.) Searchers have also discovered African rings made of ebony and animal horn.

A number of excavations have yielded fragments of colonoware, a type of ceramic vessel made by the enslaved people for food storage and preparation. Archaeologists have matched some of the designs painted on colonoware with symbols that had ritualistic importance in the Congo-Angola region of Africa. Such findings are proof that "enslaved Africans and their descendants nurtured and sustained a few aspects of an African heritage in spite of the oppressive and dehumanizing conditions of slavery," states Theresa A. Singleton, an anthropologist and archaeologist with the Smithsonian Institution.

The pottery is evidence that slaves cooked for themselves, and researchers have investigated the African influences on regional American cuisine. Some spicy southern favorites, such as jambalaya and gumbo, are cooked in one pot like many African dishes. Their names derive from the African dishes *tshimbolebole* and *kingombo,* and they were undoubtedly introduced to whites by enslaved kitchen workers.

Archaeologists have made a curious discovery in Williamsburg, Virginia, where more than half the population was black at the time of the American Revolution. The enslaved people of Williamsburg left behind spoon handles with filed edges and holes drilled in them, and scientists can only speculate about their purpose. Were they worn on strings around the neck? Did they have a spiritual meaning? Further research may provide the answers.

Even more mysterious are three charms found at The Hermitage, Andrew Jackson's home near Nashville, Tennessee. The stamped-brass charms are shaped like fists and

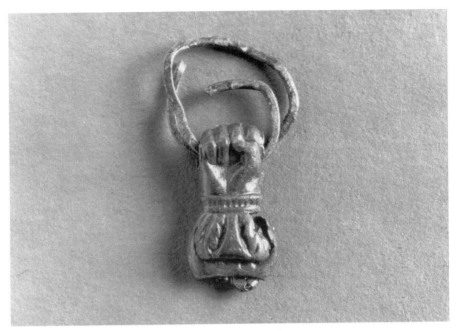

A *fist charm, one of three found at Andrew Jackson's home*   (The Hermitage: Home of President Andrew Jackson, Nashville, Tennessee)

resemble talismans used by African-based religious sects in Latin America. Hermitage archaeologist Larry McKee, Ph.D., speculates that they may be what the enslaved people called "hands"—amulets that protected them from witches' spells. The charms are proof that important aspects of slave life were kept hidden from the white masters.

Reclaiming a Heritage

The successes of the civil rights movement caused African Americans to feel a renewed pride in themselves as a people. Wanting to acknowledge their heritage, many people adopted a natural or "Afro" hairstyle and articles of African dress. Some rechristened themselves with African names. Universities added courses in African-American studies to their curriculums.

The African Burial Ground _____

In 1991, construction of a federal office building in Lower Manhattan came to a halt when workers unearthed some long-forgotten skeletons. Historians scrutinizing old maps determined that the construction workers had discovered the Negroes Burial Ground, a cemetery used by enslaved and free African Americans in 18th-century New York City. More than 3,000 African Americans lived in New York in the mid-1700s, constituting one-fifth of the city's population. Barred from using church cemeteries, they buried their dead in this municipal plot.

The 427 skeletons recovered from the site had much to teach scientists about the first Africans in the Americas. The task of studying the remains fell to Michael Blakey, Ph.D., a biological anthropologist at Howard University in Washington, D.C. As Blakey's team cleaned, measured, and examined the bones, they saw evidence of brutality. A musket ball was found with one person's remains. One woman had been struck forcefully in the face and had had her arm violently twisted. Overwork had caused muscles to tear away from bones, actually pulling off pieces of bone tissue.

Half the skeletons were children, quite a few under the age of two. Even at such a young age, their bones showed signs of hardship. Defects

Interest in the African past surged in 1976, when Alex Haley published *Roots: The Saga of an American Family.* The result of 12 years of research, *Roots* traces several generations in Haley's own family, starting with his African forebear Kunta Kinte, who survived the Middle Passage to endure a life of slavery in the American South. *Roots* earned Haley a Pulitzer Prize in 1977. Adapted as a television miniseries, it drew a larger viewing audience than any program previously aired. Both the book and the miniseries prompted Americans of all races to research their own genealogy and forced the nation to recognize the African contribution to American culture.

in tooth enamel pointed to poor nutrition in the womb and in infancy. Many of the children had suffered from rickets and other deficiency diseases.

Various clues told Blakey that some of the people whose bones he was examining had grown to adulthood in Africa. A number of the men and women had filed their teeth in a manner that signified ethnic affiliation in the Gold Coast (Ghana). One woman wore a strand of 111 beads encircling her waist in a traditional African fashion. The lid of one coffin bore a design shaped somewhat like a heart. Blakey suspects that the design is an Ashanti symbol, *sankofa*, which reminds people to study the past of their ancestors in order to understand the future.

The Africanisms uncovered at the African Burial Ground speak across the centuries to confirm that enslaved African people resisted white domination in whatever ways they could. Blakey calls those early African Americans heroes. "We would not be here were it not for them. The nation would not be there were it not for them," he says. "They had to believe that there would be a better future. How else could one survive what they survived?"

The bones will be reinterred once they have been fully studied. The African Burial Ground is now a National Historic Site, destined to be remembered by future generations.

Today, black Americans want to do more than adopt outward signs of their ties to Africa, such as hair and clothing styles. They are studying and embracing African values— standards or principles that have guided African peoples for hundreds of years. This is done, in part, through the celebration of Kwanzaa, a yearly festival held from December 26 through January 1.

A professor of black studies named Maulana Karenga conceived of Kwanzaa in 1966 as a way to restore African Americans' cultural legacy. He observed that other immigrant groups brought their holidays and feast days to the United States, but that African Americans enjoyed no such days. "Kwanzaa was created to serve as a regular communal celebration which reaffirmed and reinforced the bonds between us as a people," he explained.

The word *kwanzaa* means "first fruits of the harvest" in Swahili, a language understood in much of Africa. The African-American celebration borrows elements from harvest festivals enjoyed all over Africa. It culminates in a feast on December 31, at which participants sample recipes from the diaspora, perhaps tasting foods with an African, Caribbean, or South American flavor. Kwanzaa is a time for music and dance, for sharing readings and family stories.

An estimated 13 million people worldwide observe Kwanzaa every year. On each night of the festival, they light a candle in a *kinara,* or candle holder. The kinara holds three red candles, three green, and one black. The red candles stand for struggle, while the green ones represent hope. The black candle symbolizes the people and signifies unity. Each day of Kwanzaa is devoted to one of seven principles, or *Nguzo Saba: umoja* (unity), *kujichagulia* (self-determination), *ujima* (collective work and responsibility), *ujamaa* (cooperative economics), *nia* (purpose), *kuumba* (creativity), and *imani* (faith).

Those principles—especially unity, faith, and purpose— allowed Africans and African Americans to withstand centuries of slavery and injustice. Self-determination enabled people to retain their individuality while they were cut off from their homeland and obliged to adopt the ways of the larger white population. Through shared work and resources and through their creativity, the enslaved people and their descendants have furthered progress and enriched culture in every country of the African diaspora.

NOTES

p. 113   "provide a home for . . ." Joseph E. Harris, "The Dynamics of the Global African Diaspora," in Alusine Jalloh and Stephen E. Maizlish, eds., *The African Diaspora* (College Station, Tex.: Texas A & M University Press, 1996), p. 13.

p. 113 "Shame upon the guilty wretches . . ." Quoted in Tom W. Shick, *Behold the Promised Land: A History of Afro-American Settler Society in Nineteenth-Century Liberia* (Baltimore: The Johns Hopkins University Press, 1980). p. 3.

p. 113 "We are planted here." Quoted in Robert G. Weisbord, "The Back-to-Africa Idea," *History Today* (January 1968), p. 31.

p. 113 "We love this country . . ." Quoted in Berry and Blassingame, p. 400.

p. 113 "disappointment, discouragement, and degradation." Quoted in Weisbord, p. 32.

p. 114 "double consciousness . . . One ever feels . . ." W. E. B. Du Bois, *The Souls of Black Folk*, p. 3.

p. 115 "Wake up Ethiopia! . . ." Quoted in John Hope Franklin, *From Slavery to Freedom: A History of Negro Americans* (3d ed., New York: Alfred A. Knopf, 1967), p. 490.

p. 118 "She was early impressed . . ." Quoted in Larry G. Murphy, et al., eds., *Encyclopedia of African American Religions* (New York: Garland Publishing, 1993), p. 12.

p. 120 "enslaved Africans and their descendants . . ." Theresa A. Singleton, "The Archaeology of Slave Life," in Edward D. C. Campbell, ed., *Before Freedom Came: African-American Life in the Antebellum South* (Richmond, Va.: The Museum of the Confederacy, 1991), p. 157.

p. 123 "We would not be here . . ." "Slavery's Buried Past," *The New Explorers*, Chicago: Kurtis Productions, Ltd., and the Chicago Production Center/WTTW, 1996. Television series.

p. 124 "Kwanzaa was created to serve . . ." Maulana Karenga, "The African American Holiday of Kwanzaa: A Celebration of Family, Community, and Culture," in Herb Boyd and Robert L. Allen, eds., *Brotherman: The Odyssey of Black Men in America—An Anthology* (New York: Ballantine Books, 1995), p. 848.

Bibliography and Further Reading List

Books That Provide an Overview of the African Diaspora

Bastide, Roger. *African Civilisations in the New World*. London: C. Hurst and Company, 1967. Examines a broad range of American cultures of African descent, including maroon societies and black and Indian groups.

Berry, Mary Frances, and John W. Blassingame. *Long Memory: The Black Experience in America*. New York: Oxford University Press, 1982. African-American history from its beginnings in Africa through the civil rights movement of the 1950s and 1960s.

Chambers, Catherine. *The History of Emigration from Africa*. Danbury, Conn.: Franklin Watts, 1996. A children's book that surveys topics pertinent to diaspora studies.

Conniff, Michael L., and Thomas J. Davis. *Africans in the Americas: A History of the Black Diaspora*. New York: St. Martin's Press, 1994. Discusses slavery, emancipation, race, and politics in South America, the Caribbean, and the United States.

Harris, Joseph E., ed. *Global Dimensions of the African Diaspora*. 2d. ed. Washington, D.C.: Howard University Press, 1993. Essays by various scholars on topics ranging from the effect of the Middle Passage on Africans to Africanisms in American culture and the ongoing nature of the diaspora.

Jalloh, Alusine, and Stephen E. Maizlish, eds. *The African Diaspora.* College Station, Tex.: Texas A&M University Press, 1996. Essays on selected topics.

Pederson, Jay P., and Kenneth Estell. *African American Almanac.* Detroit, Mich.: U.X.L. 1994. This multivolume reference was prepared with young readers in mind. It may be useful for those beginning research in African-American studies.

Segal, Ronald. *The Black Diaspora: Five Centuries of the Black Experience Outside Africa.* New York: Farrar, Straus & Giroux, 1995. A comprehensive look at the African experience in the New World.

Books and Articles on Selected Topics

African History

Iliffe, John. *Africans: The History of a Continent.* Cambridge, England: Cambridge University Press, 1995. An interesting and readable account written by a British scholar.

Art

Bearden, Romare, and Harry Henderson. *Six Black Masters of American Art.* New York: Zenith Books, 1972. Profiles of outstanding African-American artists, past and present.

Perry, Regenia A. *Free Within Ourselves: African-American Artists in the collection of the National Museum of American Art.* Washington, D.C.: National Museum of American Art, Smithsonian Institution, 1992. An opportunity to learn about contemporary African-American artists and the variety of their creative work.

Wheat, Ellen Harkins. *Jacob Lawrence: American Painter.* Seattle, Wash.: University of Washington Press, 1986. A look at the life and work of a leading American artist.

The Great Migration

Marks, Carole. *Farewell—We're Good and Gone: The Great Black Migration.* Bloomington, Ind.: Indiana University Press, 1989. Describes a significant episode in African-American history.

Scott, Emmett J., comp. "Additional Letters of Negro Migrants of 1916–1918." *Journal of Negro History* 4, no. 3 (October 1919), pp. 412–65.

————. "Letters of Negro Migrants of 1916–1918." *Journal of Negro History* 4, no. 2 (July 1919), pp. 290–340. These old publications may only be available in university libraries and special collections, but the human side of the Great Migration that is expressed in these letters makes them worth looking for.

Kwanzaa

Riley, Dorothy Winbush. *The Complete Kwanzaa: Celebrating Our Cultural Harvest*. New York: HarperCollins, 1995. The origins of Kwanzaa and how it is celebrated.

Language and Literature

Crowley, Daniel J., ed. *African Folklore in the New World*. Austin, Tex.: University of Texas Press, 1977. Scholars examine how African tales have survived and evolved in the Americas.

Dillard, J. L. *Black English: Its History and Usage in the United States*. New York: Random House, 1972. Examines the structure of Black English and its similarities to other languages of the African diaspora.

Haskins, Jim. *The Harlem Renaissance*. Brookfield, Conn.: The Millbrook Press, 1996. An excellent book for young readers on an important era in American cultural history.

Johnson, Charles. *Being & Race: Black Writing Since 1970*. Bloomington, Ind.: Indiana University Press, 1988. A literary critic discusses contemporary African-American writers.

Sole, Carlos A., ed. *Latin American Writers, Vol. II*. New York: Charles Scribner's Sons, 1989. Contains a chapter on Nicolás Guillén.

Tate, Claudia. *Black Women Writers at Work*. New York: Continuum, 1989. This collection of interviews introduces readers to several African-American women who are writing today.

Music

Boyer, Horace Clarence. "Gospel Music." *Music Educators Journal* 64, no. 9 (May 1978), pp. 34–43. A professor and gospel singer explains the music he loves.

Handy, W. C. *Father of the Blues*. New York: Macmillan Co., 1941. Handy's book dates back more than a half-century, but it is still available in many libraries. Anyone interested in the blues will find it enjoyable to read.

Southern, Eileen. *The Music of Black Americans*. 3d. ed. New York: W. W. Norton, 1997. A detailed discussion of African-American music in its many forms.

Pan-Africanism and the Return to Africa

Jacques-Garvey, Amy, ed. *Philosophy and Opinions of Marcus Garvey.* New York: Atheneum, 1992. Marcus Garvey's speeches and writings collected by his wife.

Lewis, David Levering, ed. *W. E. B. Du Bois: A Reader.* New York: Henry Holt, 1995. Collected writings by the prolific African-American scholar on a wide range of topics, including pan-Africanism.

Shick, Tom W. *Behold the Promised Land: A History of Afro-American Settler Society in Nineteenth-Century Liberia.* Baltimore, Md.: The Johns Hopkins University Press, 1980. The difficult life of early settlers in Liberia.

The Panama Canal

Conniff, Michael L. *Black Labor on a White Canal: Panama, 1904–1918.* Pittsburgh, Pa.: University of Pittsburgh Press, 1985. Focuses on the lives and contributions of the black workers who built the canal.

McCullough, David. *The Path Between the Seas: The Creation of the Panama Canal, 1870–1914.* New York: Simon & Schuster, 1977. A broader history of the canal by a Pulitzer Prize–winning author.

Religion

Barnett, Milton C., ed. *Afro-American Religious History.* Durham, N.C.: Duke University Press, 1985. Writings by Richard Allen, W. E. B. Du Bois, and other prominent African Americans on religion.

González-Wippler, Migene. *Santería: The Religion.* New York: Harmony Books, 1989. An introduction to Santería and its practitioners.

Murphy, Larry G., J. Gordon Melton, and Gary L. Ward, eds. *Encyclopedia of African American Religions.* New York: Garland Publishing, 1993. A reference book filled with information on many topics pertaining to African-American religious practice and history.

Raboteau, Albert J. *A Fire in the Bones: Reflections on African-American Religious History.* Boston: Beacon Press, 1995. African-American religion in the United States in all its varied forms.

———. *Slave Religion: "The Invisible Institution" in the Antebellum South.* Oxford: Oxford University Press, 1978. How enslaved African Americans expressed their religious faith.

The Slave Trade and Slavery

Blassingame, John W. *The Slave Community: Plantation Life in the Antebellum South.* New York: Oxford University Press, 1972. A thorough description of the lives of enslaved plantation workers.

Burnside, Madeleine. *Spirits of the Passage: The Transatlantic Slave Trade in the Seventeenth Century.* New York: Simon & Schuster, 1997. A well-illustrated account of the slave trade that focuses on the *Henrietta Marie*, a sunken slave ship discovered in the Gulf of Mexico in 1972.

Campbell, Edward D. C., Jr., ed. *Before Freedom Came: African-American Life in the Antebellum South.* Richmond, Va.: The Museum of the Confederacy, 1991. This companion volume to a museum exhibit examines the lives of enslaved persons from varied perspectives.

Palmer, Colin. "African Slave Trade: The Cruelest Commerce." *National Geographic 182,* no. 3 (September 1992), pp. 63–91. A richly illustrated article that focuses on the experiences of enslaved people in Africa and the lives of their descendants in the diaspora today.

Savannah Unit, Georgia Writers' Project, Works Projects Administration. *Drums and Shadows: Survival Studies Among the Georgia Coastal Negroes.* Athens, Ga.: University of Georgia Press, 1940. These interviews with former slaves are fascinating, although the phonetic spelling of the subjects' speech appears condescending today.

Index

Italic numbers indicate illustrations.

131